Energy Conservation Construction Code of New York State

**New York State
Department of State**

Division of Code Enforcement and Administration

D1289101

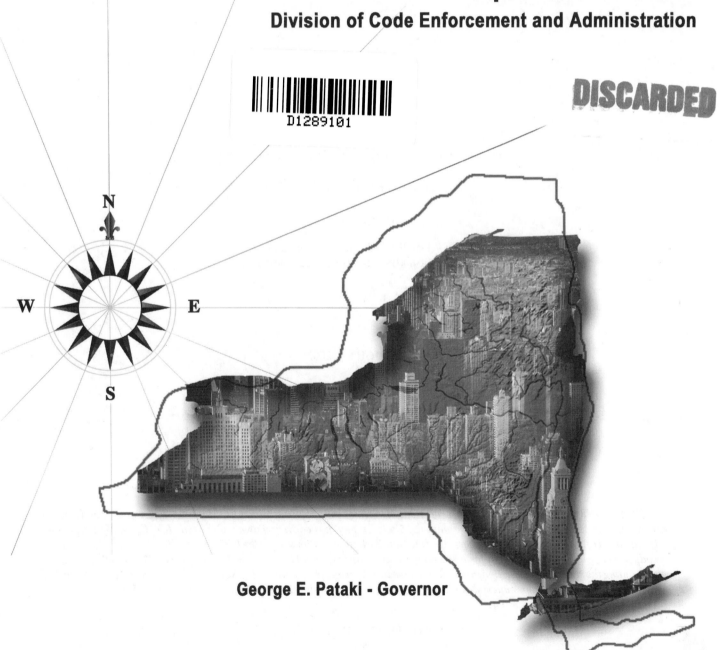

George E. Pataki - Governor

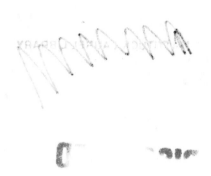

Energy Conservation Construction Code of New York State

Publication Date: May 2002

First printing

ISBN # 1-58001-083-0 (soft-cover edition)
ISBN # 1-58001-092-X (loose-leaf edition)

PRINTED IN THE U.S.A.

ACKNOWLEDGEMENTS

The Department of State gratefully acknowledges the following individuals who contributed to the development of the *Energy Conservation Construction Code of New York State*:

State Fire Prevention and Building Code Council

Randy A. Daniels, Secretary of State (Chair)
Alexander F. Treadwell, former Secretary of State (Chair 1995 - 2001)
John W. Hasper, Deputy Secretary of State (designee)
James A. Burns, State Fire Administrator
Ogden J. Clark (designee)
Antonia Coello Novello, M.D., Commissioner of Health
Barbara DeBuono, M.D., former Commissioner of Health
Richard Svenson (designee)
Linda Angello, Commissioner of Labor
James McGowan, former Commissioner of Labor
Denis Peterson (designee)
Thomas V. Ognibene, Councilman, City of New York
Roy A. Bernardi, former Mayor, City of Syracuse
Nick Altieri (designee)
James P. Griffin, Mayor, City of Olean
Christopher Young (designee)
Michael Behling, Legislator, County of Jefferson
Paul Noto, Legislator, County of Westchester
Kevin Donohue, Councilman, Town of LaGrange
Scott Wohl, Trustee, Village of Goshen
Stephen Brescia, Mayor, Village of Montgomery
Carmen Dubaldi (designee)
Gunnar Neilson, Fire Service Official
Robert G. Shibley, AIA, Registered Architect
Ronald Bugaj, Registered Architect (deceased)
Dr. James J. Yarmus, P.E., Professional Engineer
John H. Flanigan, Code Enforcement Official
Robert Hankin, Builders' representative
John J. Torpey, Trade union representative
Terence J. Moakley, Persons with disabilities representative

Department of State

Frank Milano, First Deputy Secretary of State
Dorothy M. Harris, Assistant Secretary of State (Project coordinator)
George E. Clark, Jr., Director, Division of Code Enforcement and Administration
Michael Saafir, Deputy Director
Ronald Piester, Assistant Director of Code Development
Richard DiGiovanna, Office of Counsel

Energy Conservation Construction Code Technical Subcommittee

Ray Andrews (Chair), John Addario, Michael Burnetter, Bill Richardsen (Department of State Staff)
Scott Copp, Marolyn Davenport, Mike Dewein, Mark Eggers, Joseph Fama, Nicholas Grecco, Adam Hinge, Katherine Kennedy, Michael McGowan, Stu Slote, Thomas Szekely

Administrative Task Group

Richard Thomson (Chair), James King, Thomas Romanowski, William Stewart, Robert Thompson

International Conference of Building Officials - Publications Staff

Kim Akhavan (Managing Editor), Alberto Herrera (Typesetter), Yolanda Nickoley (Typesetter), Suzane Nunes (Product Development Manager), Mary Bridges, Marje Cates, Greg Dickson, Carmel Gieson, Jessica Hoffman, Roger Mensink, Rhonda Moller, Cindy Rodriguez, Mike Tamai and Lisa Valentino

Cover Photograph

Dave Feiden

Content

The *Energy Conservation Construction Code of New York State* combines language from the 2000 *International Energy Conservation Code®*, 2001 Supplement to the *International Energy Conservation Code,* and New York modifications developed by the State Fire Prevention and Building Code Council and its Energy Code Technical Subcommittee. In addition, administrative modifications to the 2000 *International Energy Conservation Code* were developed by the Department of State's Administrative Task Group.

Marginal Markings

New York modifications to code language are indicated by NY tape ($\frac{N}{Y}$) in the margin, and New York text is underlined. Deletion of code language by New York is indicated by an arrow (➡) in the margin.

"Reserved" indicates that a section or portion of the International Code ™ has been deleted, but its number or position has been retained.

Letter Designations in Front of Section Numbers

The content of sections in this code which begin with a letter designation are maintained by another code development committee in accordance with the following: [B] = International Building Code Development Committee; [F] = International Fire Code Development Committee; [M] = International Mechanical Code Development Committee; [P] = International Plumbing Code Development Committee; [RBE] = International Residential Code Building and Energy Development Committee; [RMP] = International Residential Code Mechanical/Plumbing Development Committee; and [E] = International Energy Conservation Code Development Committee.

TABLE OF CONTENTS

CHAPTER 1

ADMINISTRATION, ENFORCEMENT
AND GENERAL REQUIREMENTS

SECTION 101
SCOPE AND GENERAL REQUIREMENTS

101.1 Title. These provisions shall be known as the *Energy Conservation Construction Code of New York State*, and shall be cited as such and will be referred to herein as "this code."

101.2 Scope. The provisions of this code shall apply to the design of building envelopes for adequate thermal resistance and low air leakage and the design and selection of mechanical, electrical, service water-heating and illumination systems and equipment which will enable effective use of energy in all new and renovated public and private building construction in New York State. It is intended that these provisions provide flexibility to permit the use of innovative approaches and techniques to achieve effective utilization of energy. This code is not intended to abridge safety, health or environmental requirements under other applicable local, state or federal laws and regulations.

101.3 Compliance. Compliance with this code shall be determined in accordance with Sections 101.3.1 through 101.3.3.

101.3.1 Residential buildings. For residential buildings, a systems approach for the entire building and its energy-using subsystems which utilizes renewable sources (Chapter 4), an approach based on performance of individual components of the building envelope (Chapter 5), an approach based on performance of the total building envelope (Chapter 5), an approach based on acceptable practice for each envelope component (Chapter 5), an approach by prescriptive specification for individual components of the building envelope (Chapter 5), or an approach based on simplified, prescriptive specification (Chapter 6) where the conditions set forth in Section 101.3.1.1 or 101.3.1.2 are satisfied. Compliance can be determined through the use of computer software developed by the United States Department of Energy (DOE) that has an allowance for HVAC tradeoffs, worksheets/compliance material based on this software and other building energy modeling or home energy rating (HERS) software approved by the Secretary of State. When using software or worksheets to show compliance, the general provisions of Chapter 5, Sections 502, 503, 504 and 505, shall be met.

101.3.1.1 Detached one- and two-family dwellings. When the glazing area does not exceed 15 percent of the gross area of exterior walls.

101.3.1.2 Type R-2, R-4 or townhouse buildings. When the glazing area does not exceed 25 percent of the gross area of exterior walls.

101.3.1.3 Electric resistance heat. Single and multi-family buildings that use electric resistance heat as the primary heat source shall use either Table 502.2.4(10),

Table 602.1(2) or DOE software for envelope compliance.

101.3.2 Commercial buildings. For commercial buildings, a prescriptive, system, or energy cost budget approach (Chapter 7) or as specified by acceptable practice (Chapter 8). Compliance can be determined through the use of computer software developed by the DOE that has an allowance for HVAC tradeoffs, worksheets/compliance material based on this software, and other building energy modeling software approved by the Secretary of State. When using software or worksheets to show compliance, the general provisions of Chapter 7 or 8 shall be met.

101.3.3 City of New York. When within the jurisdiction of New York City, counties of New York, Kings, Queens, Bronx and Richmond, the following shall apply:

1. For determination of occupancy classification and use within this code, a comparable occupancy classification may be made to the Building Code of the City of New York.
2. Where reference is made within this code to plumbing, mechanical, building, fire, electrical codes, etc., the respective Building and Electrical Codes of the City of New York shall apply.

101.4 Scope. This code establishes minimum prescriptive and performance-related regulations for the design of energy-efficient buildings and structures or portions thereof that provide facilities or shelter for public assembly, educational, business, mercantile, institutional, storage and residential occupancies, as well as those portions of factory and industrial occupancies designed primarily for human occupancy. This code thereby addresses the design of energy-efficient building envelopes and the selection and installation of energy-efficient mechanical, service water-heating, electrical distribution and illumination systems and equipment for the effective use of energy in these buildings and structures.

101.4.1 Exempt buildings. Buildings and structures indicated in Sections 101.4.1.1 through 101.4.1.3 shall be exempt from the provisions of this code. Commercial buildings provided with service water heating and/or electric lighting shall meet the applicable provisions of Chapter 7 or 8 regardless of this exempt status.

101.4.1.1 Low energy usage buildings. Buildings and structures, or portions thereof separated by building envelope assemblies from the remainder of the building, that have a peak design rate of nonrenewable energy usage less than 3.4 Btu/h per square foot (10.7 W/m^2) or 1.0 watt per square foot (10.7 W/m^2) of floor area for all purposes.

101.4.1.2 Renewable energy usage in buildings. The building design envelope provisions of this code shall not be required if the building design energy usage for heating and/or cooling can be demonstrated to be completely supplied from renewable energy sources.

101.4.2 Applicability. The provisions of this code shall apply to all matters affecting or relating to structures and premises. Where, in a specific case, different sections of this code specify different materials, methods of construction or other requirements, the most restrictive shall govern.

101.4.2.1 Existing installations. Except as otherwise provided for in this chapter, a provision in this code shall not require the removal, alteration or abandonment of, nor prevent the continued utilization and maintenance of, an existing building envelope, mechanical, service water-heating, electrical distribution or illumination system lawfully in existence at the time of the adoption of this code.

101.4.2.2 Additions. Additions shall conform to the provisions of this code as they relate to new construction without requiring the unaltered portion(s) of the existing system to comply with all of the requirements of this code. Additions shall not cause any one of the existing systems to become unsafe, hazardous or overloaded.

101.4.2.3 Historic buildings. The provisions of this code relating to alteration, repair, enlargement, restoration, relocation or moving of buildings or structures shall not be mandatory for existing buildings or structures that have been specifically determined as historically significant by the State or local governing body, or listed in the National Register of Historic Places, or that have been determined to be eligible for listing on the National Register by the State Preservation Officer.

101.4.2.4 Substantial alterations to existing buildings. This code shall apply only to that portion of a building subsystem that is replaced, provided that 50 percent or more, measured in units appropriate to that subsystem, of such building subsystem is replaced within any consecutive 12-month period.

Exceptions:

1. Installation of storm windows over existing glazing.
2. Replacement of glazing in existing sash and frame, provided the *U*-factor and solar heat gain coefficient (SHGC) will be equal to or lower than before the glass replacement.
3. Replacement of a roof membrane where either the roof sheathing or roof insulation is not exposed, or if there is existing roof insulation below the roof deck.
4. Replacement of existing doors that separate conditioned space from the exterior shall not require the installation of a vestibule or revolving door, provided that an existing vestibule that separates a conditioned space from the exterior shall not be removed.
5. Replacement of existing fenestration, provided that the area of the replacement fenestration does not exceed 50 percent of the total fenestration area

of an existing building and that the *U*-factor and solar heat gain coefficient (SHGC) will be equal to or lower than before the fenestration replacement.
6. For a subsystem that is being modified or repaired but not replaced, provided that such modifications will not result in an increase in energy usage.
7. For the relocation of existing equipment or appliance.
8. Replacement of less than 50 percent of the luminaries in a building, provided that such alterations do not increase the installed interior lighting power.
9. Repairs and/or replacements that are not substantial alterations.

101.4.2.5 Nonresidential farm buildings. The requirements of this code shall not apply to nonresidential farm buildings, including barns, sheds, poultry houses and other buildings and equipment on the premises used directly and solely for agricultural purposes.

101.4.3 Mixed occupancy. When a building houses more than one occupancy, each portion of the building shall conform to the requirements for the occupancy housed therein. Where minor accessory uses do not occupy more than 10 percent of the area of any floor of a building, the major use shall be considered the building occupancy. Buildings, other than detached one- and two-family dwellings, with a height of four or more stories above grade shall be considered commercial buildings for purposes of this code, regardless of the number of floors that are classified as residential occupancy.

101.4.4 Other laws and regulations. The provisions of this code shall not be deemed to nullify any provisions of local, state or federal laws and regulations.

SECTION 102
MATERIALS, SYSTEMS AND EQUIPMENT

102.1 General. Materials, equipment and systems shall be identified in a manner that will allow a determination of their compliance with the applicable provisions of this code.

102.2 Materials, equipment and systems installation. All insulation materials, caulking and weatherstripping, fenestration assemblies, mechanical equipment and systems components, and water-heating equipment and systems components shall be installed in accordance with the manufacturer's installation instructions.

102.3 Maintenance information. Required regular maintenance actions shall be clearly stated and incorporated on a readily accessible label. Such label shall include the title or publication number, the operation and maintenance manual for that particular model and type of product. Maintenance instructions shall be furnished for equipment that requires preventive maintenance for efficient operation.

102.4 Insulation installation. Roof/ceiling, floor, wall cavity and duct distribution systems insulation shall be installed in a manner that permits inspection of the manufacturer's *R*-value identification mark.

102.4.1 Protection of exposed foundation insulation. Insulation applied to the exterior of foundation walls and around the perimeter of slab-on-grade floors shall have a rigid, opaque and weather-resistant protective covering to prevent the degradation of the insulation's thermal performance. The protective covering shall cover the exposed area of the exterior insulation and extend a minimum of 6 inches (153 mm) below grade.

102.5 Identification. Materials, equipment and systems shall be identified in accordance with Sections 102.5.1, 102.5.2 and 102.5.3.

102.5.1 Building envelope insulation. A thermal resistance (R) identification mark shall be applied by the manufacturer to each piece of building envelope insulation 12 inches (305 mm) or greater in width.

Alternatively, the insulation installer shall provide a signed and dated certification for the insulation installed in each element of the building envelope, listing the type of insulation installations in roof/ceilings, the manufacturer and the R-value. For blown-in or sprayed insulation, the installer shall also provide the initial installed thickness, the settled thickness, the coverage area and the number of bags installed. Where blown-in or sprayed insulation is installed in walls, floors and cathedral ceilings, the installer shall provide a certification of the installed density and R-value. The installer shall post the certification in a conspicuous place on the job site.

102.5.1.1 Roof/ceiling insulation. The thickness of roof/ceiling insulation that is either blown in or sprayed shall be identified by thickness markers that are labeled in inches or millimeters installed at least one for every 300 square feet (28 m^2) throughout the attic space. The markers shall be affixed to the trusses or joists and marked with the minimum initial installed thickness and minimum settled thickness with numbers a minimum of 1 inch (25 mm) in height. Each marker shall face the attic access. The thickness of installed insulation shall meet or exceed the minimum initial installed thickness shown by the marker.

102.5.2 Fenestration product rating, certification and labeling. U-factors of fenestration products (windows, doors and skylights) shall be determined in accordance with NFRC 100 by an accredited, independent laboratory, and labeled and certified by the manufacturer. The solar heat gain coefficient (SHGC) of glazed fenestration products (windows, glazed doors and skylights) shall be determined in accordance with NFRC 200 by an accredited, independent laboratory, and labeled and certified by the manufacturer. Where a shading coefficient for a fenestration product is used, it shall be determined by converting the product's SHGC, as determined in accordance with NFRC 200, to a shading coefficient, by dividing the SHGC by 0.87. Such certified and labeled U-factors and SHGCs shall be accepted for purposes of determining compliance with the building envelope requirements of this code.

When a manufacturer has not determined product U-factor in accordance with NFRC 100 for a particular product line, compliance with the building envelope requirements of this code shall be determined by assigning such products a default U-factor in accordance with Tables 102.5.2(1) and 102.5.2(2). When an SHGC or shading coefficient is used for code compliance and a manufacturer has not determined product SHGC in accordance with NFRC 200 for a particular product line, compliance with the building envelope requirements of this code shall be determined by assigning such products a default SHGC in accordance with Table 102.5.2(3). Product features must be verifiable for the product to qualify for the default value associated with those features. Where the existence of a particular feature cannot be determined with reasonable certainty, the product shall not receive credit for that feature. Where a composite of materials from two different product types is used, the product shall be assigned the higher U-factor.

TABLE 102.5.2(1)
***U*-FACTOR DEFAULT TABLE FOR WINDOWS, GLAZED DOORS AND SKYLIGHTS**

FRAME MATERIAL AND PRODUCT TYPE[a]	SINGLE GLAZED	DOUBLE GLAZED
Metal without thermal break		
Operable (including sliding and		
swinging glass doors)	1.27	0.87
Fixed	1.13	0.69
Garden window	2.60	1.81
Curtain wall	1.22	0.79
Skylight	1.98	1.31
Site-assembled sloped/overhead glazing	1.36	0.82
Metal with thermal break		
Operable (including sliding and		
swinging glass doors)	1.08	0.65
Fixed	1.07	0.63
Curtain wall	1.11	0.68
Skylight	1.89	1.11
Site-assembled sloped/overhead glazing	1.25	0.70
Reinforced vinyl/metal clad wood		
Operable (including sliding and		
swinging glass doors)	0.90	0.57
Fixed	0.98	0.56
Skylight	1.75	1.05
Wood/vinyl/fiberglass		
Operable (including sliding and		
swinging glass doors)	0.89	0.55
Fixed	0.98	0.56
Garden window	2.31	1.61
Skylight	1.47	0.84

a. Glass block assemblies with mortar but without reinforcing or framing shall have a U-factor of 0.60.

TABLE 102.5.2(2)
***U*-FACTOR DEFAULT TABLE FOR NONGLAZED DOORS**

DOOR TYPE	WITH FOAM CORE	WITHOUT FOAM CORE
Steel doors (1.75 inches thick)	0.35	0.60

	WITHOUT STORM DOOR	WITH STORM DOOR
Wood doors (1.75 inches thick)		
Panel with 0.438-inch panels	0.54	0.36
Hollow core flush	0.46	0.32
Panel with 1.125-inch panels	0.39	0.28
Solid core flush	0.40	0.26

For SI: 1 inch = 25.4 mm.

TABLE 102.5.2(3) – 104.2   **ENFORCEMENT AND PERMITS**

TABLE 102.5.2(3)
SHGC DEFAULT TABLE FOR FENESTRATION

PRODUCT DESCRIPTION	SINGLE GLAZED				DOUBLE GLAZED			
	Clear	Bronze	Green	Gray	Clear + Clear	Bronze + Clear	Green + Clear	Gray + Clear
Metal frames								
Operable	0.75	0.64	0.62	0.61	0.66	0.55	0.53	0.52
Fixed	0.78	0.67	0.65	0.64	0.68	0.57	0.55	0.54
Nonmetal frames								
Operable	0.63	0.54	0.53	0.52	0.55	0.46	0.45	0.44
Fixed	0.75	0.64	0.62	0.61	0.66	0.54	0.53	0.52

102.5.3 Duct distribution systems insulation. A thermal resistance (*R*) identification mark shall be applied by the manufacturer in maximum intervals of no greater than 10 feet (3048 mm) to insulated flexible duct products showing the thermal performance *R*-value for the duct insulation itself (excluding air films, vapor retarders or other duct components).

102.6 Electrical energy consumption. In all buildings having individual dwelling units, provisions shall be made to determine the electrical energy consumed by each tenant by separately metering individual dwelling units.

102.7 Fireplaces. Fireplaces (solid-fuel type or ANSI Z21.50) shall be installed with tight-fitting noncombustible fireplace doors to control infiltration losses in the construction types listed here:

1. Masonry fireplaces or fireplace units designed to allow an open burn.

2. Whenever a decorative appliance (ANSI Standard Z21.60 gas-log style unit) is installed in a vented solid fuel fireplace.

3. Vented decorative gas fireplace appliances (ANSI Standard Z21.50 unit).

Fireplaces shall be provided with a source of combustion air as required by the fireplace construction provisions of the *Building Code of New York State*, the *Residential Code of New York State* or the *Building Code of the City of New York*, as applicable.

102.8 Transformers. Single-phase and three-phase dry-type and liquid-filled distribution transformers shall be selected based on rating as described in Sections 805.6.1 and 805.6.2.

SECTION 103
ALTERNATE MATERIALS—METHOD
OF CONSTRUCTION, DESIGN OR
INSULATING SYSTEMS

103.1 General. The provisions of this code are not intended to prevent the use of any material, method of construction, design or insulating system not specifically prescribed herein, provided that such construction, design or insulating systems have been approved by the State Fire Prevention and Building Code Council as meeting the intent of the code.

When within the jurisdiction of New York City, such construction, design or insulating system shall meet the intent of Building and Electrical Codes of the City of New York.

SECTION 104
CONSTRUCTION DOCUMENTS AND INSPECTIONS

104.1 General. When within the jurisdiction of New York City, refer to the Building and Electrical Codes of the City of New York for additional requirements.

104.2 Compliance documentation.

1. When plans or specifications bear the seal and signature of a licensed professional, such licensed professional shall also include a written statement that to the best of his/her knowledge, belief and professional judgment, such plans or specifications are in compliance with this code.

2. A registered design professional shall provide to the code enforcement official a written certification that the required HVAC tests, system balancing, etc., have been performed and that, in the professional opinion of the registered design professional, the system is operating as designed. The registered design professional shall retain copies of the test reports to be provided to the code enforcement official, if requested.

   Exception: One- and two-family dwelling units.

3. Whenever plans or specifications are submitted in connection with applications for building permits, such plans or specifications shall show all data and features of the building, the equipment, and the systems in sufficient detail to permit an evaluation of such plans or specifications by the code enforcement official. The plans shall clearly note the chapter(s) and method used for compliance.

4. Documents relating to the proposed construction that contain information necessary to verify compliance with this code, such as calculations, worksheets, compliance forms, vendor literature or other documents, shall be made available when requested by the code enforcement official to permit an evaluation of such documents. Compliance with specific provisions of this code shall be determined through the use of computer software, worksheets, compliance manuals and other similar materials when they have met the intent of this code. Such approved compliance methodologies and materials shall be as set forth in Section 101.3.

104.3 Information on construction documents. Construction documents shall be drawn to scale upon suitable material. Electronic media documents are permitted to be submitted. Construction documents shall be of sufficient clarity to indicate the location, nature and extent of the work proposed and show in sufficient detail pertinent data and features of the building and the equipment and systems as herein governed, including, but not limited to, design criteria, exterior envelope component materials, *U*-factors of the envelope systems, *U*-factors of fenestration products, *R*-values of insulating materials, size and type of apparatus and equipment, equipment and systems controls and other pertinent data to indicate conformance with the requirements of this code and relevant laws, ordinances, rules and regulations.

SECTION 105
ADMINISTRATION AND ENFORCEMENT

105.1 Responsibility. The administration and enforcement of the provisions of this code within any municipality shall be the responsibility of that governmental entity.

105.2 Method. This code shall be administered and enforced in the manner prescribed by applicable local law. Within the counties of New York, Kings, Queens, Bronx and Richmond, this code shall be administered and enforced in accordance with the Building and Electrical Codes of the City of New York.

SECTION 106
VALIDITY

106.1 General. If a section, subsection, sentence, clause or phrase of this code is, for any reason, held to be unconstitutional, such decision shall not affect the validity of the remaining portions of this code.

SECTION 107
REFERENCED STANDARDS

107.1 General. The standards, and portions thereof, which are referred to in this code and listed in Chapter 9, shall be considered part of the requirements of this code to the extent of such reference.

107.2 Conflicting requirements. When a section of this code and a section of a referenced standard from Chapter 9 specify different materials, methods of construction or other requirements, the provisions of this code shall apply.

SECTION 108
PENALTIES

108.1 General. Any person served with an order, pursuant to the provisions of any local law or ordinance, or to the procedures adopted pursuant to Section 381 of the Executive Law for the administration and enforcement of the *New York State Uniform Fire Prevention and Building Code*, who shall fail to comply with such order within 30 days after such service or within the time fixed by such order for compliance, whichever is greater, and any owner, builder, architect, engineer, contractor or subcontractor taking part in or assisting in the construction or use of any building, who knowingly violates any applicable provisions of this code or any lawful order of the governmental entity responsible for the administration and enforcement thereof, shall be subject to a fine of not more than $500 or to imprisonment for not more than 30 days in jail, or both. Except as otherwise provided by law, any such violation shall not be a crime, and the penalty or punishment imposed therefor shall not be deemed for any purpose a penal or criminal penalty or punishment, and shall not impose any disability upon or affect or impair the credibility as a witness, or otherwise, of any person convicted thereof.

SECTION 109
INTERPRETATION OF CODE REQUIREMENTS

109.1 General. Upon written request by a building permit applicant and/or a code enforcement official, the Secretary of State may issue an interpretation of the application of any specific requirement of this code to the proposed construction for which an application for a building permit and required plans and specifications have been filed, and concerning which there is a disagreement between the building permit applicant and the code enforcement official as to the application of such specific requirement to the proposed construction.

109.2 Procedure. A request for an interpretation shall be signed by the building permit applicant and the code enforcement official, or by one or the other, individually, and shall include the following information in order to be considered complete:

1. Name, address, and telephone number of the building permit applicant and the code enforcement official;
2. A detailed description of the proposed construction, including a copy of the building permit application and plans and specifications that have been filed by the building permit applicant with the code enforcement official, as well as any other floor plans, elevations, cross-sections, details, specifications, or construction documents necessary to describe adequately the proposed construction;
3. Identification of each requirement of this code for which an interpretation is requested;
4. A concise summary of the disagreement concerning the application of each such requirement for which an interpretation is requested; and
5. A copy of the building permit application denial if one was issued by the code enforcement official.

109.3 Incomplete information. If the request is incomplete or does not otherwise contain sufficient information necessary to issue an interpretation, the Secretary of State may request clarification of the information provided or additional information necessary to issue the requested interpretation.

109.4 Notification. Upon receipt of a complete request for an interpretation signed by only the building permit applicant or the code enforcement official, the Secretary of State shall provide written notification to the party who has not signed the request for an interpretation that such request for an interpretation has been filed with the Department of State. The party receiving such notification shall have 20 days from the date of such notification in which to provide, in writing, any comments or additional information pertaining to the request for an interpretation, provided that the Commissioner may waive this deadline when warranted by extenuating circumstances.

109.5 Issuing interpretation. The Secretary of State shall either issue the interpretation or provide notification of the intent not to issue an interpretation to the building permit applicant and the code enforcement official within 45 days of any of the following:

1. Receipt of a complete request for an interpretation signed by both the building permit applicant and the code enforcement official,

2. Receipt of comments when the request for an interpretation is signed by only one party, or

3. The expiration of the 20-day comment period when the request for an interpretation is signed by only one party.

109.6 Enforcement. Subsequent enforcement of this code with respect to the construction project for which an interpretation has been requested shall be consistent with the interpretation issued by the Secretary of State.

SECTION 110
VARIANCES AND MODIFICATIONS

110.1 General. Any standard or requirement of the code may be varied or modified, in whole or part, with regard to specific construction upon application made by or on behalf of an owner, where strict compliance with such standard or requirement would entail practical difficulty or cause any unnecessary hardship in relation to such construction, provided that any such variance or modification shall provide for alternative energy conservation standards or requirements to achieve to the extent practicable the purposes of this code.

110.2 Procedure. The petition shall consist of the application prescribed by the Department of State and all information provided by the petitioner in support of it. The petition shall be made to the Secretary of State through the Codes Division or one of its regional offices, together with copies in such number as the department may require.

CHAPTER 2
DEFINITIONS

SECTION 201
GENERAL

201.1 Scope. Unless otherwise expressly stated, the following words and terms shall, for the purposes of this code, have the meanings indicated in this chapter.

201.2 Interchangeability. Words used in the present tense include the future; words in the masculine gender include the feminine and neuter; the singular number includes the plural and the plural, the singular.

201.3 Terms defined in other codes. Where terms are not defined in this code and are defined in the *Building Code of New York State, Residential Code of New York State, Fire Code of New York State, Mechanical Code of New York State, Plumbing Code of New York State, Fuel Gas Code of New York State* or the *Property Maintenance Code of New York State*, such terms shall have meanings ascribed to them as in those codes.

201.4 Terms not defined. Where terms are not defined through the methods authorized by this section, such terms shall have ordinarily accepted meanings such as the context implies.

SECTION 202
GENERAL DEFINITIONS

ACCESSIBLE (AS APPLIED TO EQUIPMENT). Admitting close approach because not guarded by locked doors, elevation or other effective means (see "Readily accessible").

ADDITION. Any extension or increase to a building or subsystem.

ALTERATION. The replacement, modification or renovation of a subsystem.

AIR TRANSPORT FACTOR. The ratio of the rate of useful sensible heat removal from the conditioned space to the energy input to the supply and return fan motor(s), expressed in consistent units and under the designated operating conditions.

ANNUAL FUEL UTILIZATION EFFICIENCY (AFUE). The ratio of annual output energy to annual input energy which includes any nonheating season pilot input loss, and for gas or oil-fired furnaces or boilers, does not include electrical energy.

APPROVED. Approved by the code enforcement official or other authority having jurisdiction as the result of investigation and tests conducted by said official or authority, or by reason of accepted principles or tests by nationally recognized organizations.

AUTOMATIC. Self-acting, operating by its own mechanism when actuated by some impersonal influence, as, for example, a change in current strength, pressure, temperature or mechanical configuration (see "Manual").

BASEMENT WALL. The opaque portion of a wall which encloses one side of a basement and having an average below-grade area greater than or equal to 50 percent of its total wall area, including openings (see "Gross area of exterior walls").

BTU. Abbreviation for British thermal unit, which is the quantity of heat required to raise the temperature of 1 pound (0.454 kg) of water 1°F (0.56°C), (1 Btu = 1,055 J).

BUILDING. Any structure occupied or intended for supporting or sheltering any use or occupancy.

BUILDING ENVELOPE. The elements of a building which enclose conditioned spaces through which thermal energy is capable of being transferred to or from the exterior or to or from spaces exempted by the provisions of Section 101.4.1.

CODE ENFORCEMENT OFFICIAL. The officer or other designated authority charged with the administration and enforcement of this code, or a duly authorized representative.

COEFFICIENT OF PERFORMANCE (COP)—COOLING. The ratio of the rate of heat removal to the rate of energy input in consistent units, for a complete cooling system or factory-assembled equipment, as tested under a nationally recognized standard or designated operating conditions.

COEFFICIENT OF PERFORMANCE (COP)—HEAT PUMP—HEATING. The ratio of the rate of heat delivered to the rate of energy input, in consistent units, for a complete heat pump system under designated operating conditions. Supplemental heat shall not be considered when checking compliance with the heat pump equipment (COPs listed in the tables in Sections 503 and 803).

COMFORT ENVELOPE. The area on a psychrometric chart enclosing all those conditions described in Figure 2 in ASHRAE 55 as being comfortable.

COMMERCIAL BUILDING. Non-residential buildings less than four stories in height and buildings other than detached one- and two-family dwellings with a height of four or more stories above grade shall be considered commercial buildings for purposes of this code, regardless of the number of floors that are classified as residential occupancy.

CONDENSER. A heat exchanger designed to liquefy refrigerant vapor by removal of heat.

CONDENSING UNIT. A specific refrigerating machine combination for a given refrigerant, consisting of one or more power-driven compressors, condensers, liquid receivers (when required), and the regularly furnished accessories.

CONDITIONED FLOOR AREA. The horizontal projection of that portion of interior space which is contained within exterior walls and which is conditioned directly or indirectly by an energy-using system.

CONDITIONED SPACE. A heated or cooled space, or both, within a building and, where required, provided with humidification or dehumidification means so as to be capable of maintaining a space condition falling within the comfort envelope set forth in ASHRAE 55.

COOLED SPACE. Space within a building which is provided with a positive cooling supply (see "Positive cooling supply").

CRAWL SPACE WALL. The opaque portion of a wall which encloses a crawl space and is partially or totally below grade.

DEADBAND. The temperature range in which no heating or cooling is used.

DEGREE DAY, COOLING. A unit, based on temperature difference and time, used in estimating cooling energy consumption and specifying nominal cooling load of a building in summer. For any one day, when the mean temperature is more than 65°F (18°C), there are as many degree days as there are degrees Fahrenheit (Celsius) difference in temperature between the mean temperature for the day and 65°F (18°C). Annual cooling degree days (CDD) are the sum of the degree days over a calendar year.

DEGREE DAY, HEATING. A unit, based upon temperature difference and time, used in estimating heating energy consumption and specifying nominal heating load of a building in winter. For any one day, when the mean temperature is less than 65°F (18°C), there are as many degree days as there are degrees Fahrenheit (Celsius) difference in temperature between the mean temperature for the day and 65°F (18°C). Annual heating degree days (HDD) are the sum of the degree days over a calendar year.

DUCT. A tube or conduit utilized for conveying air. The air passages of self-contained systems are not to be construed as air ducts.

DUCT SYSTEM. A continuous passageway for the transmission of air that, in addition to ducts, includes duct fittings, dampers, plenums, fans and accessory air-handling equipment and appliances.

DWELLING UNIT. A single housekeeping unit comprised of one or more rooms providing complete independent living facilities for one or more persons, including permanent provisions for living, sleeping, eating, cooking and sanitation.

ECONOMIZER. A ducting arrangement and automatic control system that allows a cooling supply fan system to supply outdoor air to reduce or eliminate the need for mechanical refrigeration during mild or cold weather.

ELECTRIC RESISTANCE HEAT. Space heating systems that utilize electric resistance elements including baseboard, electric boilers, air-to-air heat pumps, and radiant and forced air units, where the total electric resistance heat capacity exceeds 1.0 W/ft^2 of the gross conditioned floor area.

ENERGY. The capacity for doing work taking a number of forms which is capable of being transformed from one into another, such as thermal (heat), mechanical (work), electrical and chemical in customary units, measured in joules (J) kilowatt-hours (kW × h) or British thermal units (Btu).

ENERGY ANALYSIS. A method for determining the annual (8,760 hours) energy use of the Proposed design and Standard design based on hour-by-hour estimates of energy use.

ENERGY COST. The total estimated annual cost for purchased energy for the building, including any demand charges, fuel adjustment factors and delivery charges applicable to the building.

ENERGY EFFICIENCY RATIO (EER). The ratio of net equipment cooling capacity in Btu/h (W) to total rate of electric input in watts under designated operating conditions. When consistent units are used, this ratio becomes equal to COP (see also "Coefficient of performance").

EVAPORATOR. That part of the system in which liquid refrigerant is vaporized to produce refrigeration.

EXTERIOR ENVELOPE. See "Building envelope."

EXTERIOR WALL. An above-grade wall enclosing conditioned space which is vertical or sloped at an angle of sixty (60) degrees (1.1 rad) or greater from the horizontal (see "Roof Assembly"). Includes between floor spandrels, peripheral edges of floors, roof and basement knee walls, dormer walls, gable end walls, walls enclosing a mansard roof, and basement walls with an average below-grade wall area which is less than 50 percent of the total opaque and non-opaque area of that enclosing side.

FENESTRATION. Skylights, roof windows, vertical windows (whether fixed or movable), opaque doors, glazed doors, glass block, and combination opaque/glazed doors.

FURNACE, DUCT. A furnace normally installed in distribution ducts of air-conditioning systems to supply warm air for heating and which depends on a blower not furnished as part of the duct furnace for air circulation.

FURNACE, WARM AIR. A self-contained, indirect-fired or electrically heated furnace that supplies heated air through ducts to spaces that require it.

GLAZING AREA. Total area of the glazed fenestration measured using the rough opening and including sash, curbing or other framing elements that enclose conditioned space. Glazing area includes the area of glazed fenestration assemblies in walls bounding conditioned basements. For doors where the daylight opening area is less than 50 percent of the door area, the glazing area is the daylight opening area. For all other doors, the glazing area is the rough opening area for the door including the door and the frame.

GROSS AREA OF EXTERIOR WALLS. The normal projection of all exterior walls, including the area of all windows and doors installed therein (see "Exterior wall").

GROSS FLOOR AREA. The sum of the areas of several floors of the building, including basements, cellars, mezzanine and intermediate floored tiers and penthouses of headroom height, measured from the exterior faces of exterior walls or from the centerline of walls separating buildings, but excluding:

1. Covered walkways, open roofed-over areas, porches and similar spaces.

2. Pipe trenches, exterior terraces or steps, chimneys, roof overhangs and similar features.

HEAT. The form of energy that is transferred by virtue of a temperature difference or a change in state of a material.

HEAT CAPACITY (HC). The amount of heat necessary to raise the temperature of a given mass by one degree. The heat capacity of a building element is the sum of the heat capacities of each of its components.

HEAT REJECTION EQUIPMENT. Equipment used in comfort cooling systems such as air cooled condensers, open cooling towers, closed-circuit cooling towers, and evaporative condensers.

HEAT PUMP. A refrigeration system that extracts heat from one substance and transfers it to another portion of the same substance or to a second substance at a higher temperature for a beneficial purpose.

HEAT TRAP. An arrangement of piping and fittings, such as elbows, or a commercially available heat trap, that prevents thermosyphoning of hot water during standby periods.

HEATED SLAB. Slab-on-grade construction in which the heating elements or hot air distribution system is in contact with or placed within the slab or the subgrade.

HEATED SPACE. Space within a building which is provided with a positive heat supply (see "Positive heating supply"). Finished living space within a basement with registers or heating devices designed to supply heat to a basement space shall automatically define that space as heated space.

HEATING SEASONAL PERFORMANCE FACTOR (HSPF). The total heating output of a heat pump during its normal annual usage period for heating, in Btu, divided by the total electric energy input during the same period, in watt hours, as determined by DOE 10 CFR Part 430, Subpart B, Test Procedures and based on Region 4.

HUMIDISTAT. A regulatory device, actuated by changes in humidity, used for automatic control of relative humidity.

HVAC. Heating, ventilating and air conditioning.

HVAC SYSTEM. The equipment, distribution network, and terminals that provide either collectively or individually the processes of heating, ventilating, or air conditioning to a building.

HVAC SYSTEM COMPONENTS. HVAC system components provide, in one or more factory-assembled packages, means for chilling or heating water, or both, with controlled temperature for delivery to terminal units serving the conditioned spaces of the building. Types of HVAC system components include, but are not limited to, water chiller packages, reciprocating condensing units and water source (hydronic) heat pumps (see "HVAC system equipment").

HVAC SYSTEM EQUIPMENT. HVAC system equipment provides, in one (single package) or more (split system) factory-assembled packages, means for air circulation, air cleaning, air cooling with controlled temperature and dehumidification, and, optionally, either alone or in combination with a heating plant, the functions of heating and humidifying. The cooling function is either electrically or heat operated and the refrigerant condenser is air, water or evaporatively cooled. Where the equipment is provided in more than one package, the separate packages shall be designed by the manufacturer to be used together. The equipment shall be permitted to provide the heating function as a heat pump or by the use of electric or fossil-fuel-fired elements. (The word "equipment" used without a modifying adjective, in accordance with common industry usage, applies either to HVAC system equipment or HVAC system components.)

INFILTRATION. The uncontrolled inward air leakage through cracks and interstices in any building element and around windows and doors of a building caused by the pressure effects of wind or the effect of differences in the indoor and outdoor air density or both.

INSULATING SHEATHING. An insulation board having a minimum thermal resistance of R-2 of the core material.

INTEGRATED PART-LOAD VALUE (IPLV). A single number of merit based on part-load EER or COP expressing part-load efficiency for air-conditioning and heat pump equipment on the basis of weighted operation at various load capacities for the equipment.

LABELED. Devices, equipment, appliances, assemblies or materials to which have been affixed a label, seal, symbol or other identifying mark of a nationally recognized testing laboratory, inspection agency or other organization concerned with product evaluation that maintains periodic inspection of the production of the above-labeled items and by whose label the manufacturer attests to compliance with applicable nationally recognized standards.

LISTED. Equipment, appliances, assemblies or materials included in a list published by a nationally recognized testing laboratory, inspection agency or other organization concerned with product evaluation that maintains periodic inspection of production of listed equipment, appliances, assemblies or material, and whose listing states either that the equipment, appliances, assemblies, or material meets nationally recognized standards or has been tested and found suitable for use in a specified manner.

LOW-VOLTAGE LIGHTING. Lighting equipment that is powered through a transformer such as cable conductor, rail conductor, and track lighting.

MANUAL. Capable of being operated by personal intervention (see "Automatic").

MULTIFAMILY DWELLING. A building containing three or more dwelling units.

NON-RESIDENTIAL FARM BUILDINGS. Farm buildings, including barns, sheds, poultry houses and other buildings and equipment on the premises, used directly and solely for agricultural puposes.

OCCUPANCY. The purpose for which a building, or portion thereof, is utilized or occupied.

OPAQUE AREAS. All exposed areas of a building envelope which enclose conditioned space, except openings for windows, skylights, doors and building service systems.

OUTDOOR AIR. Air taken from the outdoors and, therefore, not previously circulated through the system.

OZONE DEPLETION FACTOR. A relative measure of the potency of chemicals in depleting stratospheric ozone. The ozone depletion factor potential depends upon the chlorine and the bromine content and atmospheric lifetime of the chemical. The depletion factor potential is normalized such that the factor for CFC-11 is set equal to unity and the factors for the other chemicals indicate their potential relative to CFC-11.

PACKAGED TERMINAL AIR CONDITIONER (PTAC). A factory-selected wall sleeve and separate unencased combination of heating and cooling components, assemblies or sections (intended for mounting through the wall to serve a single room or zone). It includes heating capability by hot water, steam, or electricity. (For the complete technical definition, see ARI 310/380.)

PACKAGED TERMINAL HEAT PUMP. A PTAC capable of using the refrigeration system in a reverse cycle or heat pump mode to provide heat. (For the complete technical definition, see ARI 310/380.)

POSITIVE COOLING SUPPLY. Mechanical cooling deliberately supplied to a space, such as through a supply register. Also, mechanical cooling indirectly supplied to a space through uninsulated surfaces of space-cooling components, such as evaporator coil cases and cooling distribution systems which continually maintain air temperatures within the space of 85°F (29°C) or lower during normal operation. To be considered exempt from inclusion in this definition, such surfaces shall comply with the insulation requirements of this code.

POSITIVE HEAT SUPPLY. Heat deliberately supplied to a space by design, such as a supply register, radiator or heating element. Also, heat indirectly supplied to a space through uninsulated surfaces of service water heaters and space-heating components, such as furnaces, boilers and heating and cooling distribution systems which continually maintain air temperature within the space of 50°F (10°C) or higher during normal operation. To be considered exempt from inclusion in this definition, such surfaces shall comply with the insulation requirements of this code.

PROPOSED DESIGN. A description of the proposed building design used to estimate annual energy costs for determining compliance based on total building performance.

PUMP SYSTEM POWER. The sum of the nominal power demand (nameplate horsepower at nominal motor efficiency) of motors of all pumps that are required to operate at design conditions to supply fluid from the heating or cooling source to all transfer devices (e.g., coils, heat exchanger) and return it to the source.

READILY ACCESSIBLE. Capable of being reached quickly for operation, renewal or inspections, without requiring those to whom ready access is requisite to climb over or remove obstacles or to resort to portable ladders or access equipment (see "Accessible").

REFRIGERANT. A substance utilized to produce refrigeration by its expansion or vaporization or absorption.

REGISTERED DESIGN PROFESSIONAL. An individual who is a registered architect (RA) in accordance with Article 147 of the New York State Education Law or a licensed professional engineer (PE) in accordance with Article 145 of the New York State Education Law.

RENEWABLE ENERGY SOURCES. Sources of energy (excluding minerals) derived from incoming solar radiation, including natural daylighting and photosynthetic processes; from phenomena resulting therefrom, including wood, wind, waves and tides, lake or pond thermal differences; and from the internal heat of the earth, including nocturnal thermal exchanges.

REPAIR. The reconstruction or renewal of any part of an existing building for the purpose of its maintenance.

RESIDENTIAL BUILDING, R-2. Residential occupancies containing more than two dwelling units where the occupants are primarily permanent in nature such as townhouses, row houses, apartment houses, boarding houses (not transient), convents, monasteries, rectories, fraternities and sororities, dormitories, and rooming houses. For the purpose of this code, reference to Type R-2 occupancies shall refer to buildings that are three stories or less in height above grade.

RESIDENTIAL BUILDING, R-4. Residential occupancies shall include buildings arranged for occupancy as Residential Care/Assisted Living Facilities including more than five but not more than 16 occupants, excluding staff. For the purpose of this code, reference to Type R-4 occupancies shall refer to buildings that are three stories or less in height above grade.

ROOF ASSEMBLY. A roof assembly shall be considered as all roof/ceiling components of the building envelope through which heat flows, thus creating a building transmission heat loss or gain, where such assembly is exposed to outdoor air and encloses conditioned space.

The gross area of a roof assembly consists of the total interior surface of all roof/ceiling components, including opaque surfaces, dormer and bay window roofs, treyed ceilings, overhead portions of an interior stairway to an unconditioned attic, doors and hatches, glazing and skylights exposed to conditioned space, that are horizontal or sloped at an angle less than sixty (60) degrees (1.1 rad) from the horizontal (see "Exterior wall"). A roof assembly, or portions thereof, having a slope of 60 degrees (1.1 rad) or greater from the horizontal shall be considered in the gross area of exterior walls and thereby excluded from consideration in the roof assembly. Skylight shaft walls 12 inches (305 mm) in depth or greater (as measured from the ceiling plane to the roof deck) shall be considered in the gross area of exterior walls and are thereby excluded from consideration in the roof assembly.

ROOM AIR CONDITIONER. An encased assembly designed as a unit for mounting in a window or through a wall, or as a console. It is designed primarily to provide free delivery of conditioned air to an enclosed space, room or zone. It includes a prime source of refrigeration for cooling and dehumidification and means for circulating and cleaning air, and shall be permitted to also include means for ventilating and heating.

SASH CRACK. The sum of all perimeters of all window sashes, based on overall dimensions of such parts, expressed in feet. If a portion of one sash perimeter overlaps a portion of another sash perimeter, only count the length of the overlapping portions once.

SCREW LAMP HOLDERS. A lamp base that requires a screw-in-type lamp such as an incandescent or tungsten-halogen bulb.

SEASONAL ENERGY EFFICIENCY RATIO (SEER). The total cooling output of an air conditioner during its normal annual usage period for cooling, in Btu/h (W), divided by the total electric energy input during the same period, in watt-hours, as determined by DOE 10 CFR Part 430, Subpart B, Test Procedures.

SERVICE SYSTEMS. All energy-using systems in a building that are operated to provide services for the occupants or processes housed therein, including HVAC, service water heating, illumination, transportation, cooking or food preparation, laundering and similar functions.

SERVICE WATER HEATING. Supply of hot water for purposes other than comfort heating.

SIMULATION TOOL. An approved software program or calculation-based methodology that projects the hour-by-hour loads and annual energy use of a building.

SKYLIGHT. Glazing that is horizontal or sloped at an angle less than sixty (60) degrees (1.1 rad) from the horizontal (see "Glazing area").

SLAB-ON-GRADE FLOOR INSULATION. Insulation around the perimeter of the floor slab or its supporting foundation when the top edge of the floor perimeter slab is above the finished grade or 12 inches (305 mm) or less below the finished grade.

SOLAR ENERGY SOURCE. Source of natural daylighting and of thermal, chemical or electrical energy derived directly from conversion of incident solar radiation.

STANDARD DESIGN. A version of the Proposed design that meets the minimum requirements of this code and is used to determine the maximum annual energy cost requirement for compliance based on total building performance.

STANDARD TRUSS. Any construction that does not permit the roof/ceiling insulation to achieve the required R-value over the exterior walls.

SUBSTANTIAL ALTERATION. The replacement of more than 50 percent of any building subsystem within any consecutive 12-month period.

SUNROOM ADDITION. A one-story structure added to an existing dwelling with a glazing area in excess of 40 percent of the gross area of the structure's exterior walls and roof.

SYSTEM OR SUBSYSTEM. A building assembly or building set of units made up of various components that serve a specific function, including but not limited to exterior walls, windows, doors, roofs, ceilings, floors, lighting, piping, ductwork, insulation, HVAC system equipment or components, electrical appliances, and plumbing appliances.

THERMAL CONDUCTANCE. Time rate of heat flow through a body (frequently per unit area) from one of its bounding surfaces to the other for a unit temperature difference between the two surfaces, under steady conditions (Btu/h · ft^2 · °F) [W/(m^2 · K)].

THERMAL ISOLATION. A separation of conditioned spaces, between a sunroom addition and a dwelling unit, consisting of existing or new wall(s), doors, and/or windows. New wall(s), doors, and/or windows shall meet the prescriptive envelope component criteria in Table 502.2.5.

THERMAL RESISTANCE (R). The reciprocal of thermal conductance (h · ft^2 · °F/Btu) [(m^2 · K)/W].

THERMAL RESISTANCE, OVERALL (R$_o$). The reciprocal of overall thermal conductance (h · ft^2 · °F/Btu)[m^2 · K)/W]. The overall thermal resistance of the gross area or individual component of the exterior building envelope (such as roof/ceiling, exterior wall, floor, crawl space wall, foundation, window, skylight, door, opaque wall, etc.), which includes the area weighted R-values of the specific component assemblies (such as air film, insulation, drywall, framing, glazing, etc.).

THERMAL TRANSMITTANCE (U). The coefficient of heat transmission (air to air). It is the time rate of heat flow per unit area and unit temperature difference between the warm-side and cold-side air films (Btu/h · ft^2 · °F) [W/(m^2 · K)]. The U-factor applies to combinations of different materials used in series along the heat flow path, single materials that comprise a building section, cavity air spaces and surface air films on both sides of a building element.

THERMAL TRANSMITTANCE, OVERALL (U$_o$). The overall (average) heat transmission of a gross area of the exterior building envelope (Btu/h · ft.^{2} · °F) [W/(m^2 · K)]. The U$_o$-factor applies to the combined effect of the time rate of heat flow through the various parallel paths, such as windows, doors and opaque construction areas, comprising the gross area of one or more exterior building components, such as walls, floors or roof/ceilings.

THERMOSTAT. An automatic control device actuated by temperature and designed to be responsive to temperature.

TOWNHOUSE. A building not more than three stories in height consisting of multiple single-family dwelling units constructed in a group of three or more attached units, in which each unit extends from foundation to roof and with open space on at least two sides.

TRANSFORMER. Electrical equipment used to convert electric power from one voltage to another voltage.

    Dry-type transformer. A transformer in which the core and coils are in a gaseous or dry compound.

    Liquid-immersed transformer. A transformer in which the core and coils are immersed in an insulating liquid.

UNITARY COOLING AND HEATING EQUIPMENT. One or more factory-made assemblies which include an evaporator or cooling coil, a compressor and condenser combination, and which shall be permitted to include a heating function as well. When heating and cooling equipment is provided in more than one assembly, the separate assemblies shall be designed to be used together.

UNITARY HEAT PUMP. One or more factory-made assemblies which include an indoor conditioning coil, compressor(s) and outdoor coil or refrigerant-to-water heat exchanger, including means to provide both heating and cooling functions. When heat pump equipment is provided in more than one assembly, the separate assemblies shall be designed to be used together.

VENTILATION. The process of supplying or removing air by natural or mechanical means to or from any space. Such air shall be permitted to be conditioned or unconditioned.

VENTILATION AIR. That portion of supply air which comes from outside (outdoors) plus any recirculated air that has been treated to maintain the desired quality of air within a designated space (see ASHRAE 62 and definition of "Outdoor air").

WATER HEATER, INSTANTANEOUS. A water heater with an input rating of at least 4,000 Btu/h per gallon (310 W/L) stored water and a storage capacity of less than 10 gallons (38 L).

WATER HEATER, STORAGE. A water heater with an input rating less than 4,000 Btu/h per gallon (310 W/L) of stored water or storage capacity of at least 10 gallons (38 L).

WINDOW PROJECTION FACTOR. A measure of the portion of glazing that is shaded by an eave or overhang.

ZONE. A space or group of spaces within a building with heating or cooling requirements, or both, sufficiently similar so that comfort conditions can be maintained throughout by a single controlling device.

CHAPTER 3
DESIGN CONDITIONS

SECTION 301
DESIGN CRITERIA

301.1 General. The criteria of this chapter establish the design conditions for use with Chapters 4, 5, 6 and 8.

SECTION 302
THERMAL DESIGN PARAMETERS

302.1 Exterior design conditions. The following design parameters in Table 302.1 shall be used for calculations required under this code.

TABLE 302.1   ENFORCEMENT AND PERMITS

TABLE 302.1: EXTERIOR DESIGN CONDITIONS — New York State

COUNTY	WINTER DESIGN DRY-BULB TEMP.	SUMMER DESIGN DRY-BULB TEMP.	COINCIDENT WET-BULB TEMP.	HEATING DEGREE DAYS	ZONE	COUNTY	WINTER DESIGN DRY-BULB TEMP.	SUMMER DESIGN DRY-BULB TEMP.	COINCIDENT WET-BULB TEMP.	HEATING DEGREE DAYS	ZONE
Albany	-7	86	70	6894	14A	Niagara	2	85	73	6747	14A
Allegany	1	86	71	7484	15	Oneida	-5	86	70	7244	15
Bronx	13	89	73	4910	11B	Onondaga	-3	85	71	6834	14A
Broome	-2	82	69	7273	15	Ontario	1	86	71	6734	14A
Cattaraugus	2	85	73	6747	15	Orange	6	83	73	5750	12B
Cayuga	-3	85	71	6834	14A	Orleans	1	86	71	6734	14A
Chautauqua	2	85	73	6747	14A	Oswego	-3	85	71	6834	14A
Chemung	-2	87	71	6845	15	Otsego	-5	86	70	7244	15
Chenango	-2	82	69	7273	15	Putnam	6	83	73	5750	12B
Clinton	-9	83	69	7837	15	Queens	13	89	73	4910	10B
Columbia	-7	86	70	6894	14A	Rensselaer	-7	86	70	6894	14A
Cortland	-2	82	69	7273	15	Richmond	13	89	73	4910	11B
Delaware	-5	86	70	7244	15	Rockland	13	89	73	4910	12B
Dutchess	2	88	72	6391	13A	St Lawrence	-15	84	71	8255	15
Erie	2	85	73	6747	14A	Saratoga	-5	86	70	7244	14A
Essex	-15	84	71	8255	16	Schenectady	-7	86	70	6894	14A
Franklin	-15	84	71	8255	16	Schoharie	-7	86	70	6894	15
Fulton	-7	86	70	6894	15	Schuyler	-2	87	71	6845	15
Genessee	1	86	71	6734	14A	Seneca	1	86	71	6734	14A
Greene	-7	86	70	6894	14A	Steuben	1	86	71	6734	15
Hamilton	-10	85	71	7635	16	Suffolk	11	83	74	5750	11B
Herkimer	-5	86	70	7244	15	Sullivan	6	83	73	6750	15
Jefferson	-12	83	70	7540	15	Tioga	-2	87	71	6845	15
Kings	13	89	73	4910	10B	Tompkins	-2	82	69	7273	15
Lewis	-12	83	70	7540	15	Ulster	6	83	73	6750	15
Livingston	1	86	71	6734	14A	Warren	-10	85	71	7635	15
Madison	-5	86	70	7244	14A	Washington	-10	85	71	7635	15
Monroe	1	86	71	6734	14A	Wayne	1	86	71	6734	14A
Montgomery	-7	86	70	6894	14A	Westchester	7	84	73	5750	12B
Nassau	13	89	73	4910	11B	Wyoming	1	86	71	6734	14A
New York	13	89	73	4910	10B	Yates	1	86	71	6734	14A

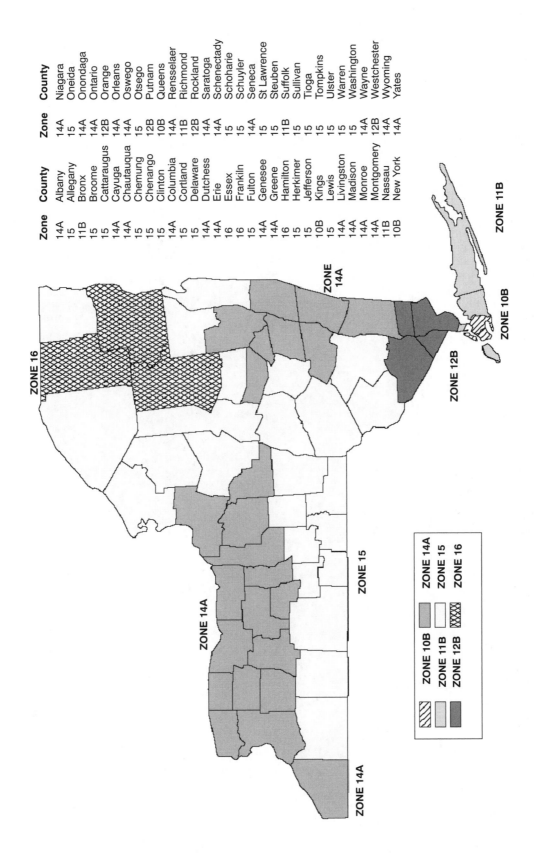

Zone	County	Zone	County
14A	Albany	14A	Niagara
15	Allegany	15	Oneida
11B	Bronx	14A	Onondaga
15	Broome	14A	Ontario
15	Cattaraugus	12B	Orange
14A	Cayuga	14A	Orleans
14A	Chautauqua	14A	Oswego
15	Chemung	15	Otsego
15	Chenango	12B	Putnam
15	Clinton	10B	Queens
14A	Columbia	14A	Rensselaer
15	Cortland	11B	Richmond
15	Delaware	12B	Rockland
14A	Dutchess	14A	Saratoga
14A	Erie	14A	Schenectady
16	Essex	15	Schoharie
16	Franklin	15	Schuyler
15	Fulton	14A	Seneca
14A	Genesee	15	St Lawrence
14A	Greene	15	Steuben
16	Hamilton	11B	Suffolk
15	Herkimer	15	Sullivan
15	Jefferson	15	Tioga
10B	Kings	15	Tompkins
15	Lewis	15	Ulster
14A	Livingston	15	Warren
14A	Madison	15	Washington
14A	Monroe	14A	Wayne
14A	Montgomery	12B	Westchester
11B	Nassau	14A	Wyoming
10B	New York	14A	Yates

FIGURE 302.1
NEW YORK

CHAPTER 4

RESIDENTIAL BUILDING DESIGN BY SYSTEMS ANALYSIS AND DESIGN OF BUILDINGS UTILIZING RENEWABLE ENERGY SOURCES

SECTION 401
SCOPE

401.1 General. This chapter establishes design criteria in terms of total energy use by a residential building, including all of its systems.

SECTION 402
SYSTEMS ANALYSIS

402.1 Energy analysis. Compliance with this chapter will require an analysis of the annual energy usage, hereinafter called an "annual energy analysis."

Exception: Chapters 5 and 6 establish criteria for different energy-consuming and enclosure elements of the building which, if followed, will eliminate the requirement for an annual energy analysis while meeting the intent of this code.

402.1.1 Standard design. A building designed in accordance with this chapter will be deemed as complying with this code if the calculated annual energy consumption is not greater than a similar building (defined as a "Standard design") whose enclosure elements and energy-consuming systems are designed in accordance with Chapter 5. Specific building envelope elements of the Standard design shall comply with Sections 402.1.1.1 through 402.1.1.4.

402.1.1.1 Exterior walls. The exterior wall assembly U-factors for the Standard design shall be selected by climate in accordance with Table 402.1.1(1).

402.1.1.2 Fenestration U-factor. The fenestration system U-factor used in the Standard design shall be selected by climate in accordance with Table 402.1.1(2).

402.1.1.3 Window area. The window area of the Standard design, inclusive of the framed sash and glazing area, shall be equal to 18 percent of the conditioned floor area of the Proposed design.

402.1.1.4 Skylights. Skylights and other nonvertical roof glazing elements shall not be included in the Standard design, and ceiling U-factors used in the Standard design shall not include such elements in their computation.

402.1.2 Proposed design. For a proposed alternate building design (defined as a "Proposed design") to be considered similar to a "Standard design," it shall utilize the same energy source(s) for the same functions and have equal conditioned floor area and the same ratio of thermal envelope area to floor area (i.e., the same geometry), exterior design conditions, occupancy, climate data, and usage operational schedule as the Standard design.

TABLE 402.1.1(1)
STANDARD DESIGN WALL ASSEMBLY U-FACTORS (U_w)

HEATING DEGREE DAYS[a]	U_w (air to air)[b]
> 13,000	0.038
9,000-12,999	0.046
6,500-8,999	0.052
4,500-6,499	0.058
3,500-4,499	0.064
2,600-3,499	0.076
< 2,600	0.085

a. From Table 302.1.
b. Including framing effects.

TABLE 402.1.1(2)
STANDARD DESIGN FENESTRATION SYSTEM U-FACTORS (U_g or U_f)

HEATING DEGREE DAYS[a]	U_g FOR SECTION 502.2.1.1 AND U_f FOR SECTION 502.2.3.1 (air to air)[b]
>13,000	0.25
9,000-12,999	0.26
6,500-8,999	0.28
4,500-6,499	0.30
3,500-4,499	0.41
2,600-3,499	0.44
700-2,599	0.47
<700	0.74

a. From Table 302.1.
b. Entire assembly, including sash.

402.1.2.1 Orientation for groups of buildings. The worst possible orientation of the Proposed design, in terms of annual energy use, considering north, northeast, east, southeast, south, southwest, west, and northwest orientations, shall be used to represent a group of otherwise identical designs.

402.1.3 Input values for residential buildings. The input values in Sections 402.1.3.1 through 402.1.3.10 shall be used in calculating annual energy performance. The requirements of this section specifically indicate which variables shall remain constant between the Standard design and Proposed design calculations. The Standard design shall be a base version of the design that directly complies with the provisions of this code. The proposed building shall be permitted to utilize a design methodology that is demonstrated through calculations to have equal or lower annual ⟵ energy use than the Standard design.

402.1.3.1 Glazing systems. The input values in Sections 402.1.3.1.1 through 402.1.3.1.5, specific to glazing systems, shall be used in calculating annual energy performance.

402.1.3.1.1 Orientation, Standard design. As a minimum, equal areas on north, east, south, and west exposures shall be assumed.

⇒ **402.1.3.1.2 Reserved.**

402.1.3.1.3 Exterior shading, Standard design. Glazing areas in the Standard design shall not be provided with exterior shading such as roof overhangs. Energy performance impacts of added exterior shading for glazing areas which are accounted for in the Proposed design for a specific building shall be permitted.

402.1.3.1.4 Fenestration system solar heat gain coefficient, Standard design. The fenestration system solar heat gain coefficient (SHGC), inclusive of framed sash and glazing area, of the glazing systems in the Standard design shall be 0.40 for HDD < 3,500 and 0.68 for HDD ≥ 3,500 during periods of mechanical heating and cooling operation. These fenestration system SHGC values shall be multiplied together with (added in series to) the interior shading values as specified in Section 402.1.3.1.5 to arrive at an overall solar heat gain coefficient for the installed glazing system.

Where the SHGC characteristics of the proposed fenestration products are not known, the default SHGC values given in Table 102.5.2(3) shall be used for the Proposed design.

402.1.3.1.5 Interior shading, Standard design and Proposed design. The same schedule of interior shading values, expressed as the fraction of the solar heat gain admitted by the fenestration system that is also admitted by the interior shading, shall be assumed for the Standard and Proposed designs.

The values used for interior shading shall be 0.70 in summer and 0.90 in winter.

Exception: South-facing solar gain apertures on passive heating Proposed designs analyzed using interior shading values for interior shading specific to those shading measures specified in the Proposed design, with values above used in the Standard design.

⇒ **402.1.3.2 Reserved.**

402.1.3.3 Heat storage (thermal mass). The following input values, specific to heat storage (thermal mass), shall be used in calculating annual energy performance:

Internal mass	8 pounds per square foot (39 kg/m^2)
Structural mass	3.5 pounds per square foot (17 kg/m^2)

402.1.3.4 Building thermal envelope—surface areas and volume. The input values in Sections 402.1.3.4.1 through 402.1.3.4.4, specific to building thermal enve-

lope surface areas, shall be used in calculating annual energy performance.

402.1.3.4.1 Floors, walls, ceiling. The Standard and Proposed designs shall have equal areas.

402.1.3.4.2 Foundation and floor type. The foundation and floor type for both the Standard and Proposed designs shall be equal.

402.1.3.4.3 Doors. The opaque door area of the Standard design shall equal that of the Proposed design and shall have a U-factor of 0.2 Btu/hr ft^2 °F [1.14 W/(m^{2}K)].

402.1.3.4.4 Building volume. The volume of both the Standard and Proposed designs shall be equal.

402.1.3.5 Heating and cooling controls. Unless otherwise specified by local codes, heating and cooling thermostats shall comply with Table 402.1.3.5 for the Standard and Proposed designs. The input values, specific to heating and cooling controls, shall be used in calculating annual energy performance.

TABLE 402.1.3.5
HEATING AND COOLING CONTROLS

Parameter	Standard design value	Proposed design value
Heating	68°F	68°F
Cooling	78°F	78°F
Set back/set up	5°F	Maximum of 5°F
Set-back/set-up duration	6 hours per day	Maximum of 6 hours per day
Number of set-back/set-up periods per unit[a]	1	Maximum of 1
Maximum number of zones per unit[a]	2	2
Number of thermostats per zone	1	1

For SI: °C = [(°F)-32]/1.8.

a. Units = Number of living units in Standard and Proposed designs.

402.1.3.6 Internal heat gains (constants). The following input values, specific to internal heat gains, shall be used in calculating annual energy performance:

Detached one- and two-family dwellings	3,000 Btu/hr (879 W) per dwelling unit
Type R-2, R-4 or townhouse residential buildings	1,500 Btu/hr (440 W) per dwelling unit

402.1.3.7 Domestic hot water (calculate, then constants). The following input values, specific to domestic hot water, shall be used in calculating annual energy performance.

Temperature set point   120°F (49°C)

Daily hot water   Gallons = $(30 \times a) + (10 \times b)$
consumption

where:

a = Number of living units in Standard and
Proposed designs.

b = Number of bedrooms in each living unit.

402.1.3.8 Site weather data (constants). The typical meteorological year (TMY2), or its "Ersatz" equivalent, from the National Oceanic and Atmospheric Administration (NOAA), or an approved equivalent, for the closest available location shall be used.

402.1.3.9 Forced-air distribution system loss factors (DLF). The heating and cooling system efficiency shall be proportionately adjusted for those portions of the ductwork located outside or inside the conditioned space using the values shown below:

System Operating Mode	Duct Location	
	Outside	Inside
Heating	0.80	1.00
Cooling	0.80	1.00

Note: Ducts located in a space that contains a positive heating or cooling supply, or both, shall be considered inside the building envelope.

Impacts from improved distribution loss factors (DLF) shall be accounted for in the Proposed design only if the entire air distribution system is specified on the construction documents to be substantially leak free, and is tested after installation to ensure that the installation is substantially leak free. "Substantially leak free" shall be defined as the condition under which the entire air distribution system (including the air handler cabinet) is capable of maintaining a 0.1-inch w.g. (25 Pa) internal pressure at 5 percent or less of the air handler's rated airflow when the return grilles and supply registers are sealed off. This test shall be conducted using methods and procedures as specified in Section 3 of the SMACNA *HVAC Air Duct Leakage Test Manual*, or by using other, similar pressurization test methods. Where test results show that the entire distribution system is substantially leak free, then seasonal DLFs shall be calculated separately for heating and cooling modes using engineering methods capable of considering the net seasonal cooling energy heat gain impacts and the net seasonal heating energy heat loss impacts that result from the portion of the thermal air distribution system that is located outside the conditioned space. Once these heating and cooling season "distribution system energy impacts" are known, then heating and cooling mode DLFs for the Proposed design shall be calculated using the following two equations:

Total Seasonal Energy = Seasonal Building Energy +
Distribution System Energy Impacts

DLF = Seasonal Building Energy/
Total Seasonal Energy

Once the DLFs for the heating and cooling seasons are known, the total "adjusted system efficiency" is calculated using the following equation:

Adjusted System Efficiency =
(Equipment Efficiency × DLF × Percent of Duct Outside) + (Equipment Efficiency × DLF × Percent of Duct Inside)

This equation shall be used to develop adjusted system efficiency for each heating and cooling system included in the Standard design. Where a single system provides both heating and cooling, efficiencies shall be calculated separately for heating and cooling modes.

402.1.3.10 Air infiltration. Annual average air changes per hour (ACH) for the Standard design shall be determined using the following equation:

ACH = Normalized Leakage × Weather Factor

where: Normalized leakage = 0.57

and   Weather factor is determined in accordance with the weather factors (*W*) given by ASHRAE 136, as taken from the weather station nearest the building site.

Where the Proposed design takes credit for reduced ACH levels, documentation of measures providing such reductions, and results of a post-construction blower-door test shall be provided to the code <u>enforcement</u> official using ASTM E 779. No energy credit shall be granted for ACH levels below 0.35.

402.1.3.11 Foundation walls. When performing annual energy analyses for buildings with insulated basement or crawl space walls, the design *U*-factors taken from Table 502.2 for these walls of the standard building shall be permitted to be decreased by accounting for the *R*-values of the adjacent soil, provided that the foundation wall *U*-factor of the proposed building also accounts for the *R*-value of the adjacent soil.

402.1.3.12 Heating and cooling system equipment efficiency, Standard design. The efficiency of the heating and cooling equipment shall meet but not exceed the minimum efficiency requirement in Section 503.2. Where the proposed design utilizes an electric resistance space heating system as the primary heating source, the Standard design shall utilize an air-cooled heat pump that meets but does not exceed the minimum efficiency requirements in Section 503.2.

402.2 Design. The Standard design, conforming to the criteria of Chapter 5 and the proposed alternative design, shall be designed on a common basis as specified in Sections 402.2.1 through 402.2.3.

402.2.1 Units of energy. The comparison shall be expressed as Btu input per square foot of gross floor area per year at building site (W/m²).

402.2.2 Equivalent energy units. If the proposed alternative design results in an increase in consumption of one energy source and a decrease in another energy source, even though similar sources are used for similar purposes, the difference in each energy source shall be converted to equivalent energy units for purposes of comparing the total energy used.

402.2.3 Site energy. The different energy sources shall be compared on the basis of energy use at the site where: 1 kWh = 3,413 Btu.

402.3 Analysis procedure. The analysis of the annual energy usage of the standard and the proposed alternative building and system design shall meet the criteria specified in Sections 402.3.1 and 402.3.2.

402.3.1 Load calculations. The building heating and cooling load calculation procedures used for annual energy consumption analysis shall be detailed to permit the evaluation of effect of factors specified in Section 402.4.

402.3.2 Simulation details. The calculation procedure used to simulate the operation of the building and its service systems through a full-year operating period shall be detailed to permit the evaluation of the effect of system design, climatic factors, operational characteristics, and mechanical equipment on annual energy usage. Manufacturer's data or comparable field test data shall be used when available in the simulation of systems and equipment. The calculation procedure shall be based upon 8,760 hours of operation of the building and its service systems and shall utilize the design methods specified in the ASHRAE *Handbook of Fundamentals.*

402.4 Calculation procedure. The calculation procedure shall include the items specified in Sections 402.4.1 through 402.4.7.

402.4.1 Design requirements. Environmental requirements as required in Chapter 3.

402.4.2 Climatic data. Coincident hourly data for temperatures, solar radiation, wind and humidity of typical days in the year representing seasonal variation.

402.4.3 Building data. Orientation, size, shape, mass, air, moisture and heat transfer characteristics.

402.4.4 Operational characteristics. Temperature, humidity, ventilation, illumination, and control mode for occupied and unoccupied hours.

402.4.5 Mechanical equipment. Design capacity, and part-load profile.

402.4.6 Building loads. Internal heat generation, lighting, equipment, and number of people during occupied and unoccupied periods.

402.4.7 Use of approved calculation tool. The same calculation tool shall be used to estimate the annual energy usage for space heating and cooling of the Standard design and the Proposed design.

402.5 Documentation. Proposed alternative designs, submitted as requests for exception to the Standard design criteria, shall be accompanied by an energy analysis comparison report.

The report shall provide technical detail on the Standard and Proposed designs and on the data used in and resulting from the comparative analysis to verify that both the analysis and the designs meet the criteria of Chapter 4.

Exception: Proposed alternative designs for residential buildings having a conditioned floor area of 5,000 square feet (464 m²) or less are exempted from the hourly analysis described in Sections 402.3 and 402.4. However, comparison of energy consumption using correlation methods based on full-year hourly simulation analysis or other engineering methods that are capable of estimating the annual heating, cooling and hot water use between the proposed alternative design and the Standard design shall be provided.

SECTION 403
SYSTEMS ANALYSIS FOR
RENEWABLE ENERGY SOURCES

403.1 General. A proposed building utilizing solar, geothermal, wind or other renewable energy sources for all or part of its energy source shall meet the requirements of Section 402, except that the provisions of this section shall also apply.

403.1.1 Equivalent energy sources. The Standard design shall use energy sources as determined by Table 403.1.1.

403.1.2 Solar energy systems, active. To qualify under this section, solar energy must be derived from a specific collection and distribution system.

403.1.3 Solar energy systems, passive. To qualify under this section, space heating energy must be derived from the absorption of solar radiation by specific building materials and its release to the conditioned space.

403.2 Documentation. Proposed alternative designs submitted as requests for exception to the Standard design criteria shall be accompanied by an energy analysis, as specified in Section 402. The report shall provide technical detail on the alternative building and system designs and on the data employed in and resulting from the comparative analysis to verify that both the analysis and the designs meet the criteria of Sections 402 and 403. The energy derived from renewable energy sources shall be clearly identified in the report.

TABLE 403.1.1 EQUIVALENT ENERGY SOURCES

| Proposed design energy source | | Standard design energy source | |
Space heating	Domestic water heating	Space heating	Domestic water heating
Some renewable energy	Some renewable energy	Non-renewable energy source used in proposed space heating design	Non-renewable energy source used in proposed domestic water heating design
Some renewable energy	All renewable energy	Non-renewable energy source used in proposed space heating design	
All renewable energy	Some renewable energy	Non-renewable energy source used in proposed domestic water heating design	
All renewable energy	All renewable energy	Heat pump meeting requirements of Table 503.2	Electric water heater meeting requirements of Table 504.2

CHAPTER 5

RESIDENTIAL BUILDING DESIGN BY COMPONENT PERFORMANCE APPROACH

SECTION 501
SCOPE

501.1 General. Residential buildings or portions thereof that enclose conditioned space shall be constructed to meet the requirements of this chapter.

SECTION 502
BUILDING ENVELOPE REQUIREMENTS

502.1 General requirements. The building envelope shall comply with the applicable provisions of Sections 502.1.1 through 502.1.5 regardless of the means of demonstrating envelope compliance as set forth in Section 502.2.

502.1.1 Moisture control. The design shall not create conditions of accelerated deterioration from moisture condensation. Frame walls, floors and ceilings not ventilated to allow moisture to escape shall be provided with an approved vapor retarder having a maximum permeance rating of 1.0 perm (5.72×10^{-8} g/Pa $\cdot$ s $\cdot$ m^2) when tested in accordance with Procedure A of ASTM E 96. The vapor retarder shall be installed on the warm-in-winter side of the thermal insulation.

Exceptions:

1. In construction where moisture or its freezing will not damage the materials.
2. Where other approved means to avoid condensation in unventilated framed wall, floor, roof and ceiling cavities are provided.

502.1.2 Masonry veneer. When insulation is placed on the exterior of a foundation supporting a masonry veneer exterior, the horizontal foundation surface supporting the veneer is not required to be insulated to satisfy any foundation insulation requirement.

502.1.3 Recessed lighting fixtures. When installed in the building envelope, recessed lighting fixtures shall meet one of the following requirements:

1. Type IC rated, manufactured with no penetrations between the inside of the recessed fixture and ceiling cavity and sealed or gasketed to prevent air leakage into the unconditioned space.
2. Type IC or non-IC rated, installed inside a sealed box constructed from a minimum 0.5-inch-thick (12.7 mm) gypsum wallboard or constructed from a pre-formed polymeric vapor barrier, or other air-tight assembly manufactured for this purpose, while maintaining required clearances of not less than 0.5

inch (12.7 mm) from combustible material and not less than 3 inches (76 mm) from insulation material.

3. Type IC rated, in accordance with ASTM E 283 admitting no more than 2.0 cubic feet per minute (cfm) (0.944 L/s) of air movement from the conditioned space to the ceiling cavity. The lighting fixture shall be tested at 1.57 psi (75 Pa) pressure difference and shall be labeled.

502.1.4 Air leakage. Provisions for air leakage shall be in accordance with Sections 502.1.4.1 and 502.1.4.2.

502.1.4.1 Window and door assemblies. Window and door assemblies installed in the building envelope shall comply with the maximum allowable infiltration rates in Table 502.1.4.1.

Exception: Site-constructed windows and doors sealed in accordance with Section 502.1.4.2.

TABLE 502.1.4.1
ALLOWABLE AIR INFILTRATION RATES[a]

WINDOWS (cfm per square foot of window area)	DOORS (cfm per square foot of door area)	
	Sliders	Swinging
0.3[b,c]	0.3	0.5[d]

For SI: 1 cfm /ft^2 = 0.00508 m^3/(s $\cdot$ m^2).

a. When tested in accordance with ASTM E 283.

b. See AAMA/WDMA 101/I.S.2.

c. See ASTM D 4099.

d. Requirement based on assembly area.

502.1.4.2 Caulking and sealants. Exterior joints, seams or penetrations in the building envelope, that are sources of air leakage, shall be sealed with durable caulking materials, closed with gasketing systems, taped or covered with moisture vapor-permeable house-wrap. Sealing materials spanning joints between dissimilar construction materials shall allow for differential expansion and contraction of the construction materials.

This includes sealing around tubs and showers, at the attic and crawl space panels, at recessed lights and around all plumbing and electrical penetrations. These are openings located in the building envelope between conditioned space and unconditioned space or between the conditioned space and the outside.

502.1.5 Fenestration solar heat gain coefficient. In locations with heating degree days (HDD) less than 3,500, the combined solar heat gain coefficient (the area-weighted average) of all glazed fenestration products (including the effects of any permanent exterior solar shading devices) in the building shall not exceed 0.4.

TABLE 502.2 – 502.2.1.1.1   RESIDENTIAL—COMPONENT PERFORMANCE APPROACH

TABLE 502.2
HEATING AND COOLING CRITERIA

ELEMENT	MODE	ZONE 10B	ZONE 11B	ZONE 12B	ZONE 13A	ZONE 14A	ZONE 15	ZONE 16
Detached one- and two-family walls	Heating or Cooling	$U_o = 0.14$	0.14	0.125	0.11	0.11	0.11	0.11
Type R-2, R-4, and townhouse walls	Heating or Cooling	$U_o = 0.215$	0.215	0.215	0.185	0.185	0.154	0.148
Roof/Ceiling	Heating or Cooling	$U_o = 0.031$	0.031	0.026	0.026	0.026	0.026	0.026
Floors over unheated space	Heating or Cooling	$U_o = 0.05$	0.05	0.05	0.05	0.05	0.05	0.05
Heated slab on grade[b]	Heating	$R = 6.5$	6.5	7	8	8	8.5	9.5
Unheated slab on grade[b]	Heating	$R = 4.5$	4.5	5	5.6	5.6	6.5	7
Basement wall[a,b]	Heating or Cooling	$U_o = 0.10$	0.1	0.096	0.096	0.096	0.09	0.06
Crawl space wall[a,b]	Heating or Cooling	$U_o = 0.06$	0.06	0.06	0.06	0.06	0.06	0.06

For SI: 1 Btu/h · ft^2 · °F = 5.678 W/(m^2 · K),   °C = [(°F)-32]/1.8.

a. Basement and crawl space wall U-factors shall be based on the wall components and surface air films. Adjacent soil shall not be considered in the determination of the U-factor.

b. Typical foundation insulation techniques can be found in the DOE Building Foundation Design Handbook.

502.2 Heating and cooling criteria. The building envelope shall meet the provisions of Table 502.2 or Table 502.2.4(10) for electric resistance heat. Compliance shall be demonstrated in accordance with Section 502.2.1, 502.2.2, 502.2.3, 502.2.4 or 502.2.5 as applicable. Energy measure trade-offs utilizing equipment exceeding the requirements of Section 503, 504 or 505 shall only use the compliance method(s) described in Chapter 4.

502.2.1 Compliance by performance on an individual component basis. Each component of the building envelope shall meet the provisions of Table 502.2 as provided in Sections 502.2.1.1 through 502.2.1.6.

502.2.1.1 Walls. The combined thermal transmittance value (U_o) of the gross area of exterior walls shall not exceed the value given in Table 502.2. Equation 5-1 shall be used to determine acceptable combinations to meet this requirement:

$$U_o = \frac{(U_w \times A_w) + (U_g \times A_g) + (U_d \times A_d)}{A_o}$$

(Equation 5-1)

where:

U_o = The average thermal transmittance of the gross area of the exterior walls.

A_o = The gross area of exterior walls.

U_w = The combined thermal transmittance of the various paths of heat transfer through the opaque exterior wall area.

A_w = Area of exterior walls that are opaque.

U_g = The combined thermal transmittance of all glazing within the gross area of exterior walls.

A_g = The area of all glazing within the gross area of exterior walls.

U_d = The combined thermal transmittance of all opaque doors within the gross area of exterior walls.

A_d = The area of all opaque doors within the gross area of exterior walls.

Notes: (1) When more than one type of wall, window or door is used, the U and A terms for those items shall be expanded into subelements as:

$(U_{w1} A_{w1}) + (U_{w2} A_{w2}) + (U_{w3} A_{w3}) + ...$ (etc.)

(Equation 5-2)

(2) Access doors or hatches in a wall assembly shall be included as a subelement of the wall assembly.

502.2.1.1.1 Steel stud framed walls. When the walls contain steel stud framing, the value of U_w used in Equation 5-1 shall be recalculated using a series path procedure to correct for parallel path thermal bridging.

The U_w for purposes of Equation 5-1 of steel stud walls shall be determined as follows:

$$U_w = \frac{1}{[R_s + (R_{ins} \times F_c)]} \qquad \textbf{(Equation 5-3)}$$

where:

R_s = The total thermal resistance of the elements comprising the wall assembly along the path of heat transfer, excluding the cavity insulation and the steel stud.

R_{ins} = The R-value of the cavity insulation.

F_c = The correction factor listed in Table 502.2.1.1.1.

Exception: Overall system tested U_w values for steel stud framed walls from approved laboratories.

TABLE 502.2.1.1.1
F_c VALUES FOR WALL SECTIONS WITH STEEL STUDS PARALLEL PATH CORRECTION FACTORS

NOMINAL STUD SIZE[a]	SPACING OF FRAMING (inches)	CAVITY INSULATION R-VALUE	CORRECTION FACTOR
2 × 4	16 o.c.	R-11	0.50
		R-13	0.46
		R-15	0.43
2 × 4	24 o.c.	R-11	0.60
		R-13	0.55
		R-15	0.52
2 × 6	16 o.c.	R-19	0.37
		R-21	0.35
2 × 6	24 o.c.	R-19	0.45
		R-21	0.43
2 × 8	16 o.c.	R-25	0.31
2 × 8	24 o.c.	R-25	0.38

For SI: 1 inch = 25.4 mm.

a. Applies to steel studs up to a maximum thickness of 0.064 inches (16 gage).

502.2.1.1.2 Mass walls. When the thermal mass of the building components is considered, the U_w for exterior walls in Section 502.2.1.1 and having a heat capacity greater than or equal to 6 Btu/ft$^2 \cdot$ °F [1.06 kJ/(m$^2 \cdot$ K)] of exterior wall area shall be less than or equal to the values in Table 502.2.1.1.2(1), 502.2.1.1.2(2) or 502.2.1.1.2(3) based on that U_w required for walls with a heat capacity less than 6 Btu/ft$^2 \cdot$ °F [1.06 kJ/(m$^2 \cdot$ K)] of exterior wall area as determined by Equation 5-1 in Section 502.2.1.1 and Table 502.2.

Note: Masonry or concrete walls having a mass greater than or equal to 30 lb/ft^2 (146 kg/m^2) of exterior wall area and solid wood walls having a mass greater than or equal to 20 lb/ft^2 (98 kg/m^2) of exterior wall area have heat capacities equal to or exceeding 6 Btu/ft$^2 \cdot$ °F [1.06 kJ/(m$^2 \cdot$ K)] of exterior wall area.

The heat capacity of the wall shall be determined as follows:

$$HC = w \times c \qquad \textbf{(Equation 5-4)}$$

where:

HC = Heat capacity of the exterior wall, Btu/ft$^2 \cdot$ °F [kJ/(m$^2 \cdot$ K)] of exterior wall area.

w = Mass of the exterior wall, lb/ft^2 (kg/m^2) of exterior wall area is the density of the exterior wall material, lb/ft^3 (kg/m^3) multiplied by the thickness of the exterior wall, ft (m).

c = Specific heat of the exterior wall material, Btu/lb $\cdot$ °F [kJ/(kg $\cdot$ K)] of exterior wall area as determined from Chapter 24 of the ASHRAE *Handbook of Fundamentals*.

502.2.1.2 Roof/ceiling. The combined thermal transmittance value (U_o) of the gross area of the roof or ceiling assembly shall not exceed the value given in Table 502.2. Equation 5-5 shall be used to determine acceptable combinations to meet this requirement.

$$U_o = \frac{(U_R \times A_R) + (U_S \times A_S)}{A_o} \qquad \textbf{(Equation 5-5)}$$

where:

U_o = The average thermal transmittance of the gross roof/ceiling area.

A_o = The gross area of the roof/ceiling assembly.

U_R = The combined thermal transmittance of the various paths of heat transfer through the opaque roof/ceiling area.

A_R = Opaque roof/ceiling assembly area.

U_s = The combined thermal transmittance of the area of all skylight elements in the roof/ceiling assembly (see Section 502.2.2.1).

A_s = The area (including frame) of all skylights in the roof/ceiling assembly (see Section 502.2.1.2.1).

Notes: (1) When more than one type of roof/ceiling or skylight is used, the U and A terms for those items shall be expanded into their subelements as:

$$(U_{R1} \times A_{R1}) + (U_{R2} \times A_{R2}) + \ldots \text{ etc. } \textbf{(Equation 5-6)}$$

(2) Access doors or hatches in a roof/ceiling assembly shall be included as a subelement of the roof/ceiling assembly.

502.2.1.2.1 Skylights. Skylight shafts, 12 inches (305 mm) in depth and greater, shall be insulated to no less than R-13 in climates 0-4,000 HDD and R-19 in climates greater than 4,000 HDD. The skylight shaft thermal performance shall not be included in the roof thermal transmission coefficient calculation.

502.2.1.3 Floors over unheated spaces. The combined thermal transmittance factor (U_o) of the gross area of floors over unheated spaces shall not exceed the value given in Table 502.2. For floors over outdoor air, i.e., overhangs, U_o-factors shall not exceed the value for roofs given in Table 502.2. Equation 5-7 shall be used to determine acceptable combinations to meet this requirement.

$$U_o = \frac{(U_{f1} \times A_{f1}) + (U_{f2} \times A_{f2}) + \ldots (U_{fn} \times A_{fn})}{A_o} \qquad \textbf{(Equation 5-7)}$$

where:

U_o = The average thermal transmittance of the gross floor area.

A_o = The gross area of the different floor assemblies.

U_{fn} = The combined thermal transmittance of the various paths of heat transfer through the nth floor assembly.

A_{fn} = The area associated with the nth floor assembly.

Notes: Access doors or hatches in a floor assembly shall be included as a subelement of the floor assembly.

TABLE 502.2.1.1.2(1)
REQUIRED U_w FOR WALL WITH A HEAT CAPACITY EQUAL TO OR EXCEEDING 6 Btu/ft^2 · °F WITH INSULATION PLACED ON THE EXTERIOR OF THE WALL MASS

N Y	HEATING DEGREE DAYS	U_w REQUIRED FOR WALLS WITH A HEAT CAPACITY LESS THAN 6 Btu/ft^2 · °F AS DETERMINED BY USING EQUATION 5-1 AND TABLE 502.2										
		0.24	0.22	0.20	0.18	0.16	0.14	0.12	0.10	0.08	0.06	0.04
	0-2,000	0.33	0.31	0.28	0.26	0.23	0.21	0.18	0.16	0.13	0.11	0.08
	2,001-4,000	0.32	0.30	0.27	0.25	0.22	0.20	0.17	0.15	0.13	0.10	0.08
	4,001-5,500	0.30	0.28	0.25	0.23	0.21	0.18	0.16	0.14	0.11	0.09	0.07
	5,501-6,500	0.28	0.26	0.23	0.21	0.19	0.17	0.15	0.12	0.10	0.08	0.06
	6,501-8,000	0.26	0.24	0.22	0.19	0.17	0.15	0.13	0.11	0.19	0.07	0.05
	>8,001	0.24	0.22	0.20	0.18	0.16	0.14	0.12	0.10	0.08	0.06	0.04

For SI: °C = [(°F)-32]/1.8, 1 Btu/ft^2 · °F = 0.176 kJ/(m^2 · K).

TABLE 502.2.1.1.2(2)
REQUIRED U_w FOR WALL WITH A HEAT CAPACITY EQUAL TO OR EXCEEDING 6 Btu/ft^2 · °F WITH INSULATION PLACED ON THE INTERIOR OF THE WALL MASS

N Y	HEATING DEGREE DAYS	U_w REQUIRED FOR WALLS WITH A HEAT CAPACITY LESS THAN 6 Btu/ft^2 · °F AS DETERMINED BY USING EQUATION 5-1 AND TABLE 502.2										
		0.24	0.22	0.20	0.18	0.16	0.14	0.12	0.10	0.08	0.06	0.04
	0-2,000	0.29	0.27	0.25	0.22	0.20	0.17	0.15	0.12	0.09	0.07	0.04
	2,001-4,000	0.28	0.26	0.24	0.21	0.19	0.16	0.14	0.12	0.09	0.07	0.04
	4,001-5,500	0.27	0.25	0.23	0.21	0.19	0.16	0.14	0.11	0.9	0.07	0.04
	5,501-6,500	0.26	0.24	0.22	0.20	0.17	0.15	0.13	0.11	0.09	0.06	0.04
	6,501-8,000	0.25	0.23	0.21	0.19	0.17	0.14	0.12	0.10	0.08	0.06	0.04
	>8,001	0.24	0.22	0.20	0.18	0.16	0.14	0.12	0.10	0.08	0.06	0.04

For SI: °C = [(°F)-32]/1.8, 1 Btu/ft^2 · °F = 0.176 kJ/(m^2 · K).

TABLE 502.2.1.1.2(3)
REQUIRED U_w FOR WALL WITH A HEAT CAPACITY EQUAL TO OR EXCEEDING 6 Btu/ft^2 · °F WITH INTEGRAL INSULATION (INSULATION AND MASS MIXED, SUCH AS A LOG WALL)

| HEATING DEGREE DAYS | U_w REQUIRED FOR WALLS WITH A HEAT CAPACITY LESS THAN 6 Btu/ft^2 · °F AS DETERMINED BY USING EQUATION 5-1 AND TABLE 502.2 | | | | | | | | | | |
	0.24	0.22	0.20	0.18	0.16	0.14	0.12	0.10	0.08	0.06	0.04
0-2,000	0.33	0.31	0.28	0.25	0.23	0.20	0.17	0.15	0.12	0.09	0.07
2,001-4,000	0.32	0.30	0.27	0.24	0.22	0.19	0.17	0.14	0.11	0.09	0.06
4,001-5,500	0.30	0.28	0.26	0.23	0.21	0.18	0.16	0.13	0.11	0.08	0.06
5,501-6,500	0.28	0.26	0.24	0.21	0.19	0.17	0.14	0.12	0.10	0.08	0.05
6,501-8,000	0.26	0.24	0.22	0.20	0.18	0.15	0.13	0.11	0.09	0.07	0.05
>8,001	0.24	0.22	0.20	0.18	0.16	0.14	0.12	0.10	0.08	0.06	0.04

For SI: °C = [(°F)-32]/1.8, 1 Btu/ft^2 · °F = 0.176 kJ/(m^2 · K).

502.2.1.4 Slab-on-grade floors. The thermal resistance of the insulation around the perimeter of the floor shall not be less than the value given in Table 502.2.

Insulation shall be of an approved type, and placed on the outside of the foundation or on the inside of a foundation wall. In climates below 6,000 annual Fahrenheit HDD, the insulation shall extend downward from the elevation of the top of the slab for a minimum distance of 24 inches (610 mm) or downward to at least the bottom of the slab and then horizontally to the interior or exterior for a minimum total distance of 24 inches (610 mm). In all climates equal to or greater than 6,000 HDD, the insulation shall extend downward from the elevation of the top of the slab for a minimum of 48 inches (1219 mm) or downward to at least the bottom of the slab and then horizontally to the interior or exterior for a minimum total distance of 48 inches (1219 mm). In all climates, horizontal insulation extending outside of the foundation shall be covered by pavement or by soil a minimum of 10 inches (254 mm) thick. The top edge of the insulation installed between the exterior wall and the edge of the interior slab shall be permitted to be cut at a 45-degree angle away from the exterior wall.

502.2.1.5 Crawl space walls. If the floor above a crawl space does not meet the requirements of Section 502.2.1.3 and the crawl space does not have ventilation openings which communicate directly with outside air, then the exterior walls of the crawl space shall have a thermal transmittance value not exceeding the value given in Table 502.2. Crawl space wall insulation shall extend vertically or vertically and horizontally a minimum total distance of 24 inches (610 mm) linearly from the outside finish ground level [see Details 502.2.1.5(1), 502.2.1.5(2) and 502.2.1.5(3) and the DOE *Foundation Design Handbook.*]

502.2.1.6 Basement walls. The exterior walls of conditioned basements shall have a transmittance value not exceeding the value given in Table 502.2 from the top of the basement wall to a depth as specified in Table 502.2.1.6 below the outside finish ground level, or to the level of the basement floor, whichever is less.

TABLE 502.2.1.6
FOUNDATION INSULATION DEPTH

Heating Degree Days	Depth Below Grade
Less than or equal to 5000	24"
5001 - 6000	24"
6001 - 7000	48"
7001 - 8000	48"
8001 - 9000	84"

502.2.2 Compliance by total building envelope performance. The building envelope design of a proposed building shall be permitted to deviate from the U_o-factors, U-factors, or R-values specified in Table 502.2, provided the total thermal transmission heat gain or loss for the proposed building envelope does not exceed the total heat gain or loss resulting from the proposed building's conformance to the values specified in Table 502.2. For basement and crawl space walls that are part of the building envelope, the U-factor of the proposed foundation shall be adjusted by the R-value of the adjacent soil where the corresponding U-factor in Table 502.2 is similarly adjusted. Heat gain or loss calculations for slab edge and basement or crawl space wall foundations shall be determined using methods consistent with the ASHRAE *Handbook of Fundamentals.*

502.2.3 Compliance by acceptable practice on an individual component basis. Each component of the building envelope shall meet the provisions of Table 502.2 as provided in Sections 502.2.3.1 through 502.2.3.6. The various walls, roof and floor assemblies described in Section 502.2.3 are typical and are not intended to be all inclusive. Other assemblies shall be permitted, provided documentation is submitted indicating the thermal transmittance value of the opaque section. Documentation shall be in accordance with accepted engineering practice.

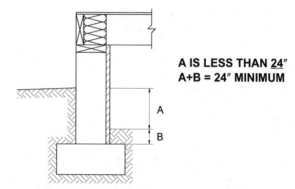

A = 24″ MINIMUM

For SI: 1 inch = 25.4 mm.

DETAIL 502.2.1.5(1)
CRAWL SPACE WALL INSULATION—INSTALLATION #1

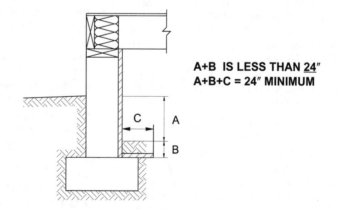

A IS LESS THAN 24″
A+B = 24″ MINIMUM

For SI: 1 inch = 25.4 mm.

DETAIL 502.2.1.5(2)
CRAWL SPACE WALL INSULATION—INSTALLATION #2

A+B IS LESS THAN 24″
A+B+C = 24″ MINIMUM

For SI: 1 inch = 25.4 mm.

DETAIL 502.2.1.5(3)
CRAWL SPACE WALL INSULATION—INSTALLATION #3[a]

a. Horizontal insulation placed on the inside ground surface shall be permitted where A + C = 24″ minimum.

502.2.3.1 Walls. The U_o of the exterior wall shall be determined in accordance with Equation 5-8.

$$U_o = \frac{(U_f \times A_f) + U_w \times (100 - A_f)}{100} \quad \textbf{(Equation 5-8)}$$

where:

U_o = The overall thermal transmittance of the gross exterior wall area.

U_f = The average thermal transmittance of the glazing area.

$$A_f = \frac{\text{Glazing Area}}{\text{Gross Exterior Wall Area}} \times 100$$

U_w = The average thermal transmittance of the opaque exterior wall area.

The U-factor for the opaque portion of the exterior wall (U_w) shall meet the provisions of Table 502.2 as determined by Equation 5-8 and be selected from Table 502.2.3.1(1), 502.2.3.1(2) or 502.2.3.1(3). The glazing U-factor (U_f) and the percentage of glazing area (A_f) shall consist of all glazed surfaces in the building envelope measured using the rough opening and including the sash, curbing and other framing elements that enclose conditioned spaces. The value of U_f shall be determined in accordance with Section 102.5.2. Opaque doors in the building envelope shall have a maximum U-factor of 0.35. One door may be exempt from this requirement.

Exceptions:

1. When the exterior wall(s) is comprised of steel stud framing members, the procedure contained in Section 502.2.1.1.1 shall be used to correct the U-factor of the opaque sections of such walls prior to selection of the appropriate acceptable practice(s) from Table 502.2.3.1(1).

2. When the thermal mass of the exterior building walls is considered, the procedure contained in Section 502.2.1.1.2 shall be used to correct the U-factor of the opaque sections of such walls prior to the selection of the appropriate acceptable practice(s) from Table 502.2.3.1(2) or 502.2.3.1(3).

502.2.3.2 Roof/ceiling. The roof/ceiling assembly shall be selected from Table 502.2.3.2 for a thermal transmittance value not exceeding the value specified for roof/ceilings in Table 502.2.

502.2.3.3 Floors over unheated spaces. The floor section over an unheated space shall be selected from Table 502.2.3.3 for the overall thermal transmittance factor (U_o) not exceeding the value specified for floors over unheated spaces in Table 502.2. For floors over outdoor air, i.e., overhangs, U_o-factors for heating shall meet the same requirement as shown for roofs/ceilings in Table 502.2.

502.2.3.4 Slab-on-grade floors. Slab-on-grade floors shall meet the provisions of Table 502.2 as determined by Section 502.2.1.4.

502.2.3.5 Crawl space walls. Where the floor above a crawl space does not meet the requirements of Section 502.2.3.3 and the crawl space does not have ventilation openings that communicate directly with outside air, then the exterior walls of the crawl space shall have a thermal transmittance value not exceeding the value given in Table 502.2. The U-factor of the exterior crawl space wall shall be determined by selecting the U-factor for the appropriate crawl space wall section from Table 502.2.3.5. Crawl space wall insulation shall extend vertically or vertically and horizontally a minimum total distance of 24 inches (610 mm) linearly from the outside finish ground level [see Details 502.2.1.5(1), 502.2.1.5(2) and 502.2.1.5(3) and the DOE *Building Foundation Design Handbook*].

502.2.3.6 Basement walls. The exterior walls of conditioned basements shall have a thermal transmittance value not exceeding the value given in Table 502.2 from the top of the basement wall to a depth as specified in Table 502.2.1.6 below grade, or to the level of the basement floor, whichever is less. The U-factor of the wall shall be determined by selecting the U-factor for the wall section from Table 502.2.3.6.

502.2.4 Compliance by prescriptive specification on an individual component basis. For buildings with a window area less than or equal to 8 percent, 12 percent, 15 percent, 18 percent, 20 percent, or 25 percent (detached one- and two-family dwellings) or 20 percent, 25 percent, or 30 percent (Type R-2, R-4 or townhouse residential buildings) of the gross exterior wall area, the thermal resistance of insulation applied to the opaque building envelope components shall be greater than or equal to the minimum R-values, and the thermal transmittance of all fenestration assemblies shall be less than or equal to the maximum U-factors shown in Table 502.2.4(1), 502.2.4(2), 502.2.4(3), 502.2.4(4), 502.2.4(5), 502.2.4(6), 502.2.4(7), 502.2.4(8), 502.2.4(9) or 502.2.4(10), as applicable. Sections 502.2.4.1 through 502.2.4.17 shall apply to the use of these tables.

TABLE 502.2.3.1(1)   RESIDENTIAL—COMPONENT PERFORMANCE APPROACH

TABLE 502.2.3.1(1)
WALL ASSEMBLIES
(U_w selected shall not exceed the U_o determined by Section 502.2.3.1 for any wall section)

WALL DETAILS[2]		TYPE AND SPACING OF FRAMING (nominal)	R-VALUE OF CAVITY INSULATION	R-VALUE OF SHEATHING	U_w[b]
Typical schedules:					
Typical interior finish— 1. Gypsum wallboard 2. Lath and plaster 3. 0.375″ minimum wood paneling	Typical exterior finish— 1. Stucco 2. Wood or plywood siding 3. Brick veneer				
WOOD STUD CONSTRUCTION INTERIOR FINISH —— EXTERIOR FINISH INSULATION —— SHEATHING		4″ Studs @ 16″ o.c.	11	non-insul	0.085
			13	non-insul	0.076
			13	3	0.064
			13	5	0.056
			13	7	0.051
			15	non-insul	0.070
			15	3	0.059
			15	5	0.053
			15	7	0.048
		6″ Studs @ 16″ o.c.	19	non-insul	0.058
			19	3	0.050
			19	5	0.046
			19	7	0.041
			21	non-insul	0.052
			21	3	0.046
			21	5	0.042
			21	7	0.038
		6″ Studs @ 24″ o.c.	21	non-insul	0.050
STEEL STUD CONSTRUCTION INTERIOR FINISH —— EXTERIOR FINISH INSULATION —— SHEATHING		4″ Studs @ 16″ o.c.	11	non-insul	0.14
			13	non-insul	0.13
		6″ Studs @ 16″ o.c.	19	non-insul	0.11
		4″ Studs @ 24″ o.c.	11	non-insul	0.12
			13	non-insul	0.11
		6″ Studs @ 24″ o.c.	19	non-insul	0.10

For SI: 1 inch = 25.4 mm.

a. Details shown are for insulation and are not complete construction details.

b. U_w calculated based on the ASHRAE *Handbook of Fundamentals*.

TABLE 502.2.3.1(2)
WALL ASSEMBLIES
(U_w selected shall not exceed the U_o determined by Section 502.2.3.1 for any wall section)

WALL DETAILS[f]	R-VALUE OR TYPE		U_w AND R_o FOR WALL THICKNESS LISTED[a]			
			6″	8″	10″	12″
Plain concrete masonry Block construction	No insulation No interior finish	U_w R_o	0.37 2.70	0.33 3.03	0.31 3.23	0.30 3.33
	Loose fill in cores No interior finish	U_w R_o	0.18 5.56	0.13 7.69	0.11 9.09	0.09 11.11
	No insulation Interior finish	U_w R_o	0.24 4.17	0.23 4.35	0.22 4.55	0.21 4.76
	No insulation Foil-backed gypsum board interior finish	U_w R_o	0.18 5.56	0.17 5.88	0.16 6.25	0.16 6.25
	1″ extruded polystyrene Interior finish	U_w R_o	0.13 7.69	0.13 7.69	0.12 8.33	0.12 8.33
	2″ expanded polystyrene Interior finish	U_w R_o	0.09 11.11	0.09 11.11	0.09 11.11	0.09 11.11
	2″ extruded polystyrene Interior finish	U_w R_o	0.08 12.50	0.08 12.50	0.08 12.50	0.08 12.50
	2″ polyisocyanurate Interior finish	U_w R_o	0.06 16.67	0.06 16.67	0.06 16.67	0.06 16.67
	R-11, 2×3 studs Interior finish	U_w R_o	0.07 14.29	0.07 14.29	0.07 14.29	0.07 14.29
	R-13, 2×3 studs Interior finish	U_w R_o	0.06 16.67	0.06 16.67	0.06 16.67	0.06 16.67
	R-19, 2×4 studs Interior finish	U_w R_o	0.05 20.00	0.05 20.00	0.05 20.00	0.05 20.00
	MULTI-WYTHE WALLS		U_w AND R_o FOR WALL THICKNESS LISTED[b,c,d,e]			
			8″	10″	12″	14″
Cavity insulation and interior finish: 0.5-inch gypsum board on furring strips	No insulation No interior finish	U_w R_o	0.32 3.13	0.26 3.85	0.24 4.17	0.22 4.55
	Loose fill in cavity No interior finish	U_w R_o	NA NA	0.12 8.33	0.12 8.33	0.11 9.09
	Loose fill Interior finish	U_w R_o	0.11 9.03	0.10 10.00	0.10 10.00	0.10 10.00
	Loose fill foil-backed gypsum board Interior finish	U_w R_o	0.10 10.00	0.09 11.11	0.09 11.11	0.09 11.11
	1″ expanded polystyrene in cavity Interior finish	U_w R_o	NA NA	0.13 7.69	0.12 8.33	0.12 8.33
	2″ expanded polystyrene in cavity Interior finish	U_w R_o	NA NA	0.08 12.50	0.08 12.50	0.08 12.50
	1″ extruded polystyrene in cavity Interior finish	U_w R_o	NA NA	0.11 9.09	0.11 9.09	0.11 9.09
	2″ extruded polystyrene in cavity Interior finish	U_w R_o	NA NA	0.07 14.29	0.07 14.29	0.07 14.29
	1″ polyisocyanurate in cavity Interior finish	U_w R_o	NA NA	0.08 12.50	0.08 12.50	0.08 12.50
	2″ polyisocyanurate in cavity Interior finish	U_w R_o	NA NA	0.05 20.00	0.05 20.00	0.05 20.00
	1″expanded polystyrene in cavity foil-backed gypsum board Interior finish	U_w R_o	NA NA	0.09 11.11	0.09 11.11	0.09 11.11
	1″ extruded polystyrene in cavity foil-backed gypsum board Interior finish	U_w R_o	NA NA	0.08 12.50	0.08 12.50	0.08 12.50

For SI: 1 inch = 25.4 mm, 1 pound per cubic foot = 0.1572 kg/m³.

a. The U_w values are for blocks made with concrete having a density of 80 pounds per cubic foot; for other densities, the U_w must be calculated based on the R-values provided in NCMA 6-1A or the ASHRAE *Handbook of Fundamentals*.

b. 8″, composite wall: 4″, dense outer wythe and hollow-unit inner wythe.

c. 10″ cavity wall: 4″ dense outer wythe, 2″ air space and 4″ hollow-unit inner wythe.

d. 12″ cavity wall: 4″ dense outer wythe, 2″ air space and 6″ hollow-unit inner wythe.

e. 14″ cavity wall: 4″ dense outer wythe, 2″ air space and 8″ hollow-unit inner wythe.

f. Refer to drawings in Tables 502.2.3.1(1) and 502.2.3.1(3).

NA = Not Applicable.

TABLE 502.2.3.1(3)

RESIDENTIAL—COMPONENT PERFORMANCE APPROACH

TABLE 502.2.3.1(3)
WALL ASSEMBLIES
(U_w selected shall not exceed the U_o determined by Section 502.2.3.1 for any wall section)

WALL DETAILS[d]		R-VALUE OF INSULATION	U_w	R_o
Interior finish 0.25″ gypsum board applied on furring strips				
BRICK MASONRY CONSTRUCTION WITH LOOSE FILL		Solid grout in space	0.38	2.63
		2″ space with loose fill R-4	0.16	6.25
		4″ space with loose fill R-8	0.10	10.00
BRICK MASONRY CONSTRUCTION WITH INSULATION		4	0.12	8.33
		6	0.09	11.11
		11	0.07	14.29
NORMAL-WEIGHT CONCRETE CONSTRUCTION		4	0.18	5.56
		6	0.13	7.69
		7	0.12	8.33
		11	0.08	12.50
LIGHTWEIGHT CONCRETE CONSTRUCTION		4	0.17	5.88
		6	0.12	8.33
		7	0.11	9.09
		11	0.08	12.50
INSULATING CONCRETE FORM SYSTEM (ICF)[c]		12	0.07	13.55
		15	0.06	16.55
		16	0.06	17.55
		17	0.05	18.55
		20	0.05	21.55
		22	0.04	23.55

For SI: 1 inch = 25.4 mm.

a. The R-value listed is the sum of the values for the exterior and interior insulation layers.

b. The manufacturer shall be consulted for the U_w and R_o values if the insulated concrete form system (ICF) uses metal form ties to connect the interior and exterior insulation layers.

c. These values shall be permitted to be used for concrete masonry wall assemblies with exterior and interior insulation layers.

d. Details shown are for insulation and are not complete construction details.

TABLE 502.2.3.2
ROOF/CEILING ASSEMBLIES
(U_r selected shall not exceed the value specified in Section 502.2.3.2)

ROOF DETAILS[a, b]	R-VALUE OF INSULATION[b]	U_r	R_o
Typical interior finish schedule: 1. Gypsum wallboard 2. Lath & plaster			
	19	0.05	20.00
	22	0.04	25.00
	30	0.03	33.33
	38	0.025	40.00
	19	0.05	20.00
	22	0.04	25.00
	30	0.03	33.33
	38	0.025	40.00
	Wood decking		
	9	0.08	12.50
	Plywood		
	10	0.08	12.50
	19	0.05	20.00
	30	0.03	33.33

a. Details shown are for insulation and are not complete construction details.
b. Skylights not exceeding one percent of the roof are permitted.
c. Insulation installed between joints.

TABLE 502.2.3.3
FLOOR ASSEMBLIES
(U_r selected shall not exceed the U_o specified in Section 502.2.3.3)

FLOOR DETAILS[a]	R-VALUE OF INSULATION	U_r	R_o
	No insulation	0.32	3.13
	7	0.11	9.09
	11	0.08	12.50
	19	0.05	20.00

a. Details shown are for insulation and are not complete construction details.

TABLE 502.2.3.5

RESIDENTIAL—COMPONENT PERFORMANCE APPROACH

TABLE 502.2.3.5
CRAWL SPACE FOUNDATION WALL ASSEMBLIES
(U-factor selected shall not exceed the U-factor determined by Section 502.2.3.5)

WALL DETAILS[a]	R-VALUE OF INSULATION	U-FACTOR
WOOD FOUNDATION	11	0.10
	13	0.09
	19	0.06
CONCRETE/MASONRY FOUNDATION—INTERIOR INSULATION	5	0.15
	10	0.08
	11	0.08
	13	0.07
	19	0.05
CONCRETE/MASONRY FOUNDATION—EXTERIOR INSULATION	3	0.20
	5	0.15
	10	0.08
	15	0.06
INSULATING CONCRETE FORM SYSTEM (ICF)[b, c, d]	12	0.08
	15	0.06
	16	0.06
	17	0.06
	20	0.05
	22	0.04

a. Details shown are for insulation and are not complete construction details.

b. The R-value listed is the sum of the values for the exterior and interior insulation layers.

c. The manufacturer shall be consulted for the U-factor if the insulated concrete form system (ICF) uses metal form ties to connect the interior and exterior insulation layers.

d. These values shall be permitted to be used for concrete masonry wall assemblies with exterior and interior insulation layers.

TABLE 502.2.3.6
BASEMENT FOUNDATION WALL ASSEMBLIES
(U-factor selected shall not exceed the U-factor determined by Section 502.2.3.6)

WALL DETAILS[a]	R-VALUE OF INSULATION	U-FACTOR
WOOD FOUNDATION	11	0.08
	13	0.08
	19	0.06
CONCRETE/MASONRY FOUNDATION—INTERIOR INSULATION	5	0.15
	6.5	0.12
	10	0.08
	11	0.08
	19	0.06
CONCRETE/MASONRY FOUNDATION—EXTERIOR INSULATION	3	0.20
	5	0.15
	10	0.09
	15	0.06
INSULATING CONCRETE FORM SYSTEM (ICF)[b, c, d]	12	0.07
	15	0.06
	16	0.06
	17	0.05
	20	0.05
	22	0.04

a. Details shown are for insulation and are not complete construction details.

b. The R-value listed is the sum of the values for the exterior and interior insulation layers.

c. The manufacturer shall be consulted for the U-factor if the insulated concrete form system (ICF) uses metal form ties to connect the interior and exterior insulation layers.

d. These values shall be permitted to be used for concrete masonry wall assemblies with exterior and interior insulation layers.

TABLE 502.2.4(1) – TABLE 502.2.4(2)   RESIDENTIAL—COMPONENT PERFORMANCE APPROACH

TABLE 502.2.4(1)
PRESCRIPTIVE BUILDING ENVELOPE REQUIREMENTS, DETACHED ONE- AND TWO-FAMILY DWELLINGS
WINDOW AREA 8 PERCENT OF GROSS EXTERIOR WALL AREA

| HEATING DEGREE DAYS | MAXIMUM | MINIMUM | | | | | |
	Glazing U-Factor	Ceiling R-value	Exterior wall R-value	Floor R-value	Basement wall R-value	Slab perimeter R-value and depth	Crawl space wall R-value
0-499	any	R-13	R-11	R-11	R-0	R-0	R-0
500-999	any	R-19	R-11	R-11	R-0	R-0	R-4
1,000-1,499	any	R-19	R-11	R-11	R-0	R-0	R-5
1,500-1,999	any	R-19	R-11	R-11	R-5	R-0	R-5
2,000-2,499	0.90	R-19	R-11	R-11	R-5	R-0	R-6
2,500-2,999	0.70	R-26	R-11	R-11	R-5	R-0	R-6
3,000-3,499	0.70	R-26	R-11	R-13	R-5	R-0	R-6
3,500-3,999	0.65	R-30	R-11	R-13	R-6	R-2, 2 ft.	R-7
4,000-4,499	0.59	R-30	R-11	R-15	R-8	R-2, 2 ft.	R-9
4,500-4,999	0.55	R-30	R-13	R-15	R-8	R-2, 2 ft.	R-12
5,000-5,499	0.52	R-30	R-13	R-19	R-9	R-7, 2 ft.	R-16
5,500-5,999	0.45	R-38	R-13	R-19	R-9	R-7, 2 ft.	R-16
6,000-6,499	0.45	R-38	R-16	R-19	R-10	R-7, 4 ft.	R-16
6,500-6,999	0.43	R-38	R-16	R-19	R-10	R-7, 4 ft.	R-16
7,000-8,499	0.42	R-38	R-16	R-19	R-11	R-8, 4 ft.	R-16
8,500-8,999	0.42	R-38	R-16	R-19	R-16	R-8, 4 ft.	R-16
9,000-12,999	0.42	R-38	R-16	R-19	R-16	R-11, 4 ft.	R-16

For SI: 1 foot = 304.8 mm.

TABLE 502.2.4(2)
PRESCRIPTIVE BUILDING ENVELOPE REQUIREMENTS, DETACHED ONE- AND TWO-FAMILY DWELLINGS
WINDOW AREA 12 PERCENT OF GROSS EXTERIOR WALL AREA

| HEATING DEGREE DAYS | MAXIMUM | MINIMUM | | | | | |
	Glazing U-Factor	Ceiling R-value	Exterior wall R-value	Floor R-value	Basement wall R-value	Slab perimeter R-value and depth	Crawl space wall R-value
0-449	any	R-13	R-11	R-11	R-0	R-0	R-0
500-999	any	R-19	R-11	R-11	R-0	R-0	R-4
1,000-1,499	0.75	R-19	R-11	R-11	R-0	R-0	R-5
1,500-1,999	0.75	R-19	R-11	R-11	R-4	R-0	R-5
2,000-2,499	0.65	R-19	R-13	R-11	R-5	R-0	R-5
2,500-2,999	0.60	R-26	R-13	R-13	R-5	R-0	R-5
3,000-3,499	0.60	R-30	R-13	R-15	R-6	R-0	R-6
3,500-3,999	0.60	R-30	R-13	R-19	R-8	R-4, 2 ft.	R-10
4,000-4,499	0.55	R-38	R-13	R-19	R-9	R-4, 2 ft.	R-12
4,500-4,999	0.50	R-38	R-14	R-19	R-9	R-5, 2 ft.	R-16
5,000-5,499	0.45	R-38	R-16	R-19	R-9	R-6, 2 ft.	R-16
5,500-5,999	0.45	R-38	R-17	R-19	R-9	R-6, 2 ft.	R-16
6,000-6,499	0.40	R-38	R-18	R-19	R-10	R-6, 4 ft.	R-16
6,500-6,999	0.40	R-49	R-21	R-19	R-10	R-7, 4 ft.	R-17
7,000-8,499	0.40	E-49	R-21	R-19	R-10	R-9, 4 ft.	R-17
8,500-8,999	0.40	R-49	R-21	R-19	R-16	R-9, 4 ft.	R-17
9,000-12,999	0.40	R-49	R-21	R-19	R-16	R-11, 4 ft.	R-17

For SI: 1 foot = 304.8 mm.

TABLE 502.2.4(3)
PRESCRIPTIVE BUILDING ENVELOPE REQUIREMENTS, DETACHED ONE- AND TWO-FAMILY DWELLINGS
WINDOW AREA 15 PERCENT OF GROSS EXTERIOR WALL AREA

HEATING DEGREE DAYS	MAXIMUM	MINIMUM					
	Glazing *U*-Factor	Ceiling *R*-value	Exterior wall *R*-value	Floor *R*-value	Basement wall *R*-value	Slab perimeter *R*-value and depth	Crawl space wall *R*-value
0-499	any	R-13	R-11	R-11	R-0	R-0	R-0
500-999	0.90	R-19	R-11	R-11	R-0	R-0	R-4
1,000-1,499	0.75	R-19	R-11	R-11	R-0	R-0	R-5
1,500-1,999	0.75	R-26	R-13	R-11	R-5	R-0	R-5
2,000-2,499	0.65	R-30	R-13	R-11	R-5	R-0	R-6
2,500-2,999	0.60	R-30	R-13	R-19	R-6	R-4, 2 ft.	R-7
3,000-3,499	0.55	R-30	R-13	R-19	R-7	R-4, 2 ft.	R-8
3,500-3,999	0.50	R-30	R-13	R-19	R-8	R-5, 2 ft.	R-10
4,000-4,499	0.45	R-38	R-13	R-19	R-8	R-5, 2 ft.	R-11
4,500-4,999	0.45	R-38	R-16	R-19	R-9	R-6, 2 ft.	R-17
5,000-5,499	0.45	R-38	R-18	R-19	R-9	R-6, 2 ft.	R-17
5,500-5,999	0.40	R-38	R-18	R-21	R-10	R-9, 2 ft.	R-19
6,000-6,499	0.35	R-38	R-18	R-21	R-10	R-9, 4 ft.	R-20
6,500-6,999	0.35	R-49	R-21	R-21	R-11	R-11, 4 ft.	R-20
7,000-8,499	0.35	R-49	R-21	R-21	R-11	R-13, 4 ft.	R-20
8,500-8,999	0.35	R-49	R-21	R-21	R-18	R-14, 4 ft.	R-20
9,000-12,999	0.35	R-49	R-21	R-21	R-19	R-18, 4 ft.	R-20

For SI: 1 foot = 304.8 mm.

TABLE 502.2.4(4)
PRESCRIPTIVE BUILDING ENVELOPE REQUIREMENTS, DETACHED ONE- AND TWO-FAMILY DWELLINGS
WINDOW AREA 18 PERCENT OF GROSS EXTERIOR WALL AREA

HEATING DEGREE DAYS	MAXIMUM	MINIMUM					
	Glazing *U*-Factor	Ceiling *R*-value	Exterior wall *R*-value	Floor *R*-value	Basement wall *R*-value	Slab perimeter *R*-value and depth	Crawl space wall *R*-value
0-499	0.80	R-19	R-11	R-11	R-0	R-0	R-0
500-999	0.75	R-19	R-11	R-11	R-0	R-0	R-4
1,000-1,499	0.70	R-26	R-13	R-11	R-0	R-0	R-5
1,500-1,999	0.65	R-30	R-13	R-11	R-5	R-0	R-5
2,000-2,499	0.55	R-30	R-13	R-11	R-5	R-0	R-6
2,500-2,999	0.52	R-30	R-13	R-19	R-6	R-0	R-7
3,000-3,499	0.50	R-38	R-13	R-19	R-7	R-0	R-8
3,500-3,999	0.46	R-38	R-13	R-19	R-8	R-6, 2 ft.	R-11
4,000-4,499	0.40	R-38	R-13	R-19	R-9	R-6, 2 ft.	R-13
4,500-4,999	0.37	R-38	R-15	R-19	R-9	R-6, 2 ft.	R-16
5,000-5,499	0.37	R-38	R-16	R-19	R-9	R-7, 2 ft.	R-17
5,500-5,999	0.37	R-38	R-19	R-19	R-10	R-8, 2 ft.	R-17
6,000-6,499	0.34	R-49	R-22	R-19	R-10	R-8, 4 ft.	R-17
6,500-6,999	0.33	R-49	R-22	R-25	R-11	R-14, 4 ft.	R-19
7,000-8,499	0.33	R-49	R-25	R-30	R-15	Note a	R-25
8,500-8,999	0.33	R-49	R-25	R-30	R-19	Note a	R-25
9,000-12,999	0.33	R-49	R-25	R-30	R-19	Note a	R-25

For SI: 1 foot = 304.8 mm.

a. See Section 502.2.4.13.

TABLE 502.2.4(5) – TABLE 502.2.4(6)   RESIDENTIAL—COMPONENT PERFORMANCE APPROACH

TABLE 502.2.4(5)
PRESCRIPTIVE BUILDING ENVELOPE REQUIREMENTS, DETACHED ONE- AND TWO-FAMILY DWELLINGS
WINDOW AREA 20 PERCENT OF GROSS EXTERIOR WALL AREA

HEATING DEGREE DAYS	MAXIMUM	MINIMUM					
	Glazing *U*-Factor	Ceiling *R*-value	Exterior wall *R*-value	Floor *R*-value	Basement wall *R*-value	Slab perimeter *R*-value and depth	Crawl space wall *R*-value
0-499	0.80	R-19	R-11	R-11	R-0	R-0	R-0
500-999	0.75	R-30	R-13	R-11	R-0	R-0	R-4
1,000-1,499	0.70	R-30	R-13	R-11	R-0	R-0	R-5
1,500-1,999	0.60	R-30	R-13	R-11	R-5	R-0	R-5
2,000-2,499	0.52	R-38	R-13	R-11	R-5	R-0	R-6
2,500-2,999	0.50	R-38	R-13	R-19	R-6	R-0	R-7
3,000-3,499	0.46	R-38	R-13	R-19	R-7	R-0	R-9
3,500-3,999	0.42	R-38	R-13	R-19	R-8	R-6, 2 ft.	R-10
4,000-4,499	0.37	R-38	R-13	R-19	R-9	R-6, 2 ft.	R-13
4,500-4,999	0.37	R-38	R-16	R-19	R-9	R-6, 2 ft.	R-16
5,000-5,499	0.36	R-38	R-19	R-19	R-9	R-6, 2 ft.	R-16
5,500-5,999	0.33	R-49	R-20	R-19	R-10	R-7, 2 ft.	R-17
6,000-6,499	0.31	R-49	R-24	R-19	R-10	R-7, 4 ft.	R-17
6,500-6,999	0.30	R-49	R-26	R-21	R-11	R-10, 4 ft.	R-17
7,000-8,499	0.30	R-49	R-26	R-21	R-11	R-12, 4 ft.	R-19
8,500-8,999	0.30	R-49	R-26	R-21	R-19	R-12, 4 ft.	R-19
9,000-12,999	0.30	R-49	R-26	R-21	R-19	R-16, 4 ft.	R-19

For SI: 1 foot = 304.8 mm.

TABLE 502.2.4(6)
PRESCRIPTIVE BUILDING ENVELOPE REQUIREMENTS, DETACHED ONE- AND TWO-FAMILY DWELLINGS
WINDOW AREA 25 PERCENT OF GROSS EXTERIOR WALL AREA

HEATING DEGREE DAYS	MAXIMUM	MINIMUM					
	Glazing *U*-Factor	Ceiling *R*-value	Exterior wall *R*-value	Floor *R*-value	Basement wall *R*-value	Slab perimeter *R*-value and depth	Crawl space wall *R*-value
0-499	0.70	R-30	R-11	R-11	R-0	R-0	R-0
500-999	0.65	R-30	R-13	R-11	R-0	R-0	R-4
1,000-1,499	0.55	R-30	R-13	R-11	R-0	R-0	R-5
1,500-1,999	0.52	R-30	R-13	R-13	R-6	R-0	R-6
2,000-2,499	0.50	R-38	R-13	R-19	R-8	R-0	R-10
2,500-2,999	0.46	R-38	R-16	R-19	R-6	R-0	R-7
3,000-3,499	0.45	R-38	R-19	R-19	R-7	R-0	R-9
3,500-3,999	0.41	R-38	R-19	R-19	R-8	R-6, 2 ft.	R-10
4,000-4,499	0.37	R-38	R-19	R-19	R-9	R-6, 2 ft.	R-13
4,500-4,999	0.33	R-38	R-19	R-19	R-9	R-6, 2 ft.	R-17
5,000-5,499	0.29	R-38	R-19	R-19	R-9	R-6, 2 ft.	R-17
5,500-5,999	0.27	R-38	R-19	R-21	R-10	Note a	R-22
6,000-6,499	0.25	R-49	R-19	R-21	R-10	R-9, 4 ft.	R-20
6,500-6,999	0.25	R-49	R-19	R-30	R-14	Note a	Note a
7,000-8,499	0.25	R-49	R-19	R-30	R-15	Note a	Note a
8,500-8,999	0.25	R-49	R-19	R-30	R-28	Note a	Note a
9,000-12,999	0.25	R-49	R-19	R-30	R-28	Note a	Note a

For SI: 1 foot = 304.8 mm.

a. See Section 502.2.4.13.

TABLE 502.2.4(7)
PRESCRIPTIVE BUILDING ENVELOPE REQUIREMENTS, TYPE R-2, R-4 OR TOWNHOUSE RESIDENTIAL BUILDINGS
WINDOW AREA 20 PERCENT OF GROSS EXTERIOR WALL AREA

HEATING DEGREE DAYS	MAXIMUM	MINIMUM					
	Glazing *U*-Factor	Ceiling *R*-value	Exterior wall *R*-value	Floor *R*-value	Basement wall *R*-value	Slab perimeter *R*-value and depth	Crawl space wall *R*-value
0-499	any	R-13	R-11	R-11	R-0	R-0	R-0
500-999	any	R-19	R-11	R-11	R-0	R-0	R-5
1,000-1,499	any	R-19	R-11	R-11	R-0	R-0	R-5
1,500-1,999	0.85	R-19	R-11	R-11	R-5	R-0	R-5
2,000-2,499	0.70	R-19	R-11	R-11	R-5	R-0	R-5
2,500-2,999	0.55	R-30	R-13	R-11	R-5	R-0	R-5
3,000-3,499	0.55	R-30	R-13	R-11	R-5	R-0	R-5
3,500-3,999	0.55	R-30	R-13	R-11	R-5	R-0	R-5
4,000-4,499	0.55	R-38	R-13	R-11	R-5	R-0	R-5
4,500-4,999	0.50	R-26	R-11	R-13	R-6	R-0	R-7
5,000-5,499	0.50	R-26	R-13	R-11	R-5	R-0	R-6
5,500-5,999	0.50	R-30	R-13	R-11	R-5	R-0	R-6
6,000-6,499	0.50	R-26	R-13	R-19	R-9	R-5, 4 ft.	R-14
6,500-6,999	0.45	R-30	R-13	R-19	R-10	R-7, 4 ft.	R-16
7,000-8,499	0.35	R-38	R-16	R-19	R-11	R-9, 4 ft.	R-18
8,500-8,999	0.35	R-38	R-16	R-19	R-17	R-10, 4 ft.	R-18
9,000-12,999	Note a	Note a	Note a	Note a	Note a	Note a	Note a

For SI: 1 foot = 304.8 mm.

a. See Section 502.2.4.13.

TABLE 502.2.4(8)
PRESCRIPTIVE BUILDING ENVELOPE REQUIREMENTS, TYPE R-2, R-4 OR TOWNHOUSE RESIDENTIAL BUILDINGS
WINDOW AREA 25 PERCENT OF GROSS EXTERIOR WALL AREA

HEATING DEGREE DAYS	MAXIMUM	MINIMUM					
	Glazing *U*-Factor	Ceiling *R*-value	Exterior wall *R*-value	Floor *R*-value	Basement wall *R*-value	Slab perimeter *R*-value and depth	Crawl space wall *R*-value
0-499	any	R-13	R-11	R-11	R-0	R-0	R-0
500-999	any	R-19	R-11	R-11	R-0	R-0	R-5
1,000-1,499	any	R-19	R-11	R-11	R-0	R-0	R-5
1,500-1,999	0.85	R-19	R-11	R-11	R-5	R-0	R-5
2,000-2,499	0.70	R-19	R-11	R-11	R-5	R-0	R-5
2,500-2,999	0.55	R-30	R-13	R-11	R-5	R-0	R-5
3,000-3,499	0.55	R-30	R-13	R-11	R-5	R-0	R-5
3,500-3,999	0.55	R-30	R-13	R-11	R-5	R-0	R-5
4,000-4,499	0.54	R-30	R-13	R-11	R-5	R-0	R-5
4,500-4,999	0.53	R-30	R-13	R-11	R-5	R-0	R-6
5,000-5,499	0.52	R-30	R-13	R-11	R-5	R-0	R-6
5,500-5,999	0.51	R-30	R-13	R-11	R-6	R-0	R-6
6,000-6,499	0.51	R-30	R-13	R-19	R-10	R-7, 4 ft.	R-16
6,500-6,999	0.45	R-30	R-13	R-19	R-10	R-7, 4 ft.	R-16
7,000-8,499	0.35	R-38	R-16	R-19	R-11	R-9, 4 ft.	R-18
8,500-8,999	0.35	R-38	R-16	R-19	R-17	R-10, 4 ft.	R-18
9,000-12,999	Note a	Note a	Note a	Note a	Note a	Note a	Note a

For SI: 1 foot = 304.8 mm.

a. See Section 502.2.4.13.

TABLE 502.2.4(9) – 502.2.4.8   RESIDENTIAL—COMPONENT PERFORMANCE APPROACH

TABLE 502.2.4(9)
PRESCRIPTIVE BUILDING ENVELOPE REQUIREMENTS, TYPE R-2, R-4 OR TOWNHOUSE RESIDENTIAL BUILDINGS
WINDOW AREA 30 PERCENT OF GROSS EXTERIOR WALL AREA

HEATING DEGREE DAYS	MAXIMUM	MINIMUM					
	Glazing *U*-Factor	Ceiling *R*-value	Exterior wall *R*-value	Floor *R*-value	Basement wall *R*-value	Slab perimeter *R*-value and depth	Crawl space wall *R*-value
0-499	0.90	R-13	R-11	R-11	R-0	R-0	R-0
500-999	0.75	R-19	R-11	R-11	R-0	R-0	R-3
1,000-1,499	0.70	R-19	R-11	R-11	R-0	R-0	R-4
1,500-1,999	0.65	R-26	R-11	R-11	R-5	R-0	R-5
2,000-2,499	0.57	R-38	R-13	R-11	R-5	R-0	R-6
2,500-2,999	0.47	R-38	R-13	R-19	R-7	R-0	R-8
3,000-3,499	0.47	R-38	R-13	R-19	R-7	R-0	R-9
3,500-3,999	0.46	R-38	R-13	R-19	R-8	R-4, 2 ft.	R-9
4,000-4,499	0.46	R-38	R-13	R-19	R-9	R-6, 2 ft	R-13
4,500-4,999	0.45	R-38	R-13	R-19	R-9	R-6, 2 ft	R-15
5,000-5,499	0.45	R-38	R-13	R-19	R-10	R-8, 2 ft.	R-18
5,500-5,999	0.44	R-38	R-13	R-19	R-10	R-8, 2 ft.	R-18
6,000-6,499	0.44	R-38	R-19	R-19	R-10	R-8, 4 ft.	R-18
6,500-6,999	0.38	R-38	R-19	R-19	R-10	R-8, 4 ft.	R-18
7,000-8,499	0.32	R-49	R-21	R-30	R-18	Note a	Note a
8,500-8,999	0.32	R-49	R-21	R-30	Note a	Note a	Note a
9,000-12,999	Note a	Note a	Note a	Note a	Note a	Note a	Note a

For SI: 1 foot = 304.8 mm.

a. See Section 502.2.4.13.

TABLE 502.2.4(10)
ENVELOPE INSULATION *R*-VALUES AND GLAZING *U*-FACTOR REQUIREMENTS
FOR RESIDENCES USING ELECTRIC RESISTANCE HEATING

Building element	Single and multi-family houses
Roof/ceiling	R-49
Wall (above grade)[b]	R-26
Glazing *U*-factor[a]	0.31
Floor over unheated space or crawl space wall	R-30
Basement wall	R-19, 7 ft. or to top of slab
Slab edge	R-15, 4 ft.

a. Maximum Allowable Glazing: 15% of the wall area.

b. Opaque doors shall have a maximum *U*-factor of 0.35.

502.2.4.1 Walls. The sum of the thermal resistance of cavity insulation plus insulating sheathing (if used) shall meet or exceed the "Exterior wall *R*-value."

502.2.4.2 Wood construction only. The tables shall only be used for wood construction.

502.2.4.3 Window area. The actual window area of a proposed design shall be computed using the rough opening area of all skylights, above-grade windows and, where the basement is conditioned space, any basement windows.

502.2.4.4 Window area, exempt. One percent of the total window area computed under Section 502.2.4.3 shall be exempt from the "Glazing *U*-factor" requirement.

502.2.4.5 Truss/rafter construction. "Ceiling *R*-value" assumes standard truss or rafter construction. Where raised-heel trusses or other construction techniques are employed to obtain the full height of ceiling insulation over the exterior wall top plate, R-30 shall be permitted to be used where R-38 is required in the table, and R-38 shall be permitted to be used where R-49 is required.

502.2.4.6 Doors. Opaque doors in the building envelope shall have a maximum *U*-factor of 0.35. One door may be exempt from this requirement.

502.2.4.7 Ceilings. "Ceiling *R*-value" shall be required for flat or "cathedral" (inclined) ceilings.

502.2.4.8 Floors. "Floor *R*-value" shall apply to floors over unconditioned spaces. A floor over outside air shall meet the requirement for "Ceiling *R*-value."

502.2.4.9 Basement walls. Basement wall insulation shall be installed in accordance with Section 502.2.1.6.

502.2.4.10 Unheated slabs. Slab perimeter insulation shall be installed in accordance with Section 502.2.1.4.

502.2.4.11 Heated slabs. R-2 shall be added to the "Slab Perimeter *R*-Value" where the slab is heated.

502.2.4.12 Crawl space walls. "Crawl Space Wall *R*-value" shall apply to unventilated crawl spaces only. Crawl space insulation shall be installed in accordance with Section 502.2.1.5.

502.2.4.13 Tables not applicable. The particular climate range indicated by Note a in Tables 502.2.4(4), 502.2.4(6), 502.2.4(7), 502.2.4(8) and 502.2.4(9) shall not be used with the indicated envelope component(s) to demonstrate compliance under Section 502.2.4.

502.2.4.14 Climates greater than 13,000 HDD. These tables shall not be used for climates greater than or equal to 13,000 HDD.

502.2.4.15 Fenestration solar heat gain coefficient. In locations with HDD less than 3,500, fenestration products shall also meet the requirements of Section 502.1.5.

502.2.4.16 Steel-framed wall construction. Where steel framing is used in wall construction, the wall assembly shall meet the equivalent wall cavity and sheathing *R*- values in Table 502.2.4.16(1) or 502.2.4.16(2), based on the "on-center" (o.c.) dimension of the steel studs and the required *R*-value for wood-framed walls determined in accordance with Section 502.2.4, and utilizing any combination of cavity and sheathing insulation set off by commas in Table 502.2.4.16(1) or 502.2.4.16(2).

502.2.4.17 High-mass wall construction. Exterior walls constructed of high-mass materials having heat capacity greater than or equal to 6 Btu/ft^2 · °F [1.06 kJ/(m^2 · K)] of exterior wall area shall meet the equivalent insulation *R*-values in Table 502.2.4.17(1) or 502.2.4.17(2), based on the placement of the insulation, the HDD of the building location, and the required *R*-value for wood-framed walls determined in accordance with Section 502.2.4.

502.2.5 Prescriptive path for additions and window replacements. As an alternative to demonstrating compliance with Section 402 or 502.2, additions with a conditioned floor area less than 500 square feet (46.5 m^2) to existing single-family residential buildings and structures shall meet the prescriptive envelope component criteria in Table 502.2.5 for the designated heating degree days (HDD) applicable to the location. The *U*-factor of each individual fenestration product (windows, doors and skylights) shall be used to calculate an area-weighted average fenestration product *U*-factor for the addition, which shall not exceed the applicable listed values in Table 502.2.5. For additions, other than sunroom additions, the total area of fenestration products shall not exceed 40 percent of the gross wall and roof area of the addition. The *R*-values for opaque thermal envelope components shall be equal to or greater than the applicable listed values in Table 502.2.5. Replacement fenestration products (where the entire unit, including the frame, sash and glazing, is replaced) shall meet the prescriptive fenestration *U*-factor criteria in Table 502.2.5 for the designated HDD

applicable to the location. Conditioned sunroom additions shall be served by a separate heating or cooling system, or shall be controlled as a separate zone of the existing system. Fenestration products used in additions and as replacement windows in accordance with this section shall also meet the requirements of Section 502.1.5 in locations with HDD less than 3,500.

Exception: Replacement skylights shall have a maximum *U*-factor of 0.50 when installed in any location above 1,999 HDD.

TABLE 502.2.4.16(1)
16-INCH O.C. STEEL-FRAMED WALL EQUIVALENT *R*-VALUES

WOOD-FRAMED WALL *R*-VALUE[a]	EQUIVALENT STEEL-FRAMED WALL CAVITY AND SHEATHING *R*-VALUE
R-11	R-0+R-9, R-11+R-4, R-15+R-3, R-21+R-2
R-13	R-11+R-5, R-15+R-4, R-21+R-3
R-14	R-11+R-6, R-13+R-5, R-19+R-4
R-15	R-11+R-6, R-15+R-5, R-19+R-4
R-16	R-11+R-8, R-15+R-7, R-21+R-6
R-17	R-11+R-9, R-13+R-8, R-19+R-7
R-18	R-11+R-9, R-15+R-8, R-21+R-7
R-19	R-11+R-10, R-13+R-9, R-19+R-8, R-25+R-7
R-20	R-11+R-10, R-13+R-9, R-19+R-8
R-21	R-13+R-10, R-19+R-9, R-25+R-8
R-22	R-13+R-10, R-19+R-9
R-24	R-19+R-10, R-25+R-9
R-25	R-19+R-10
R-26	R-19+R-11, R-21+R-10

For SI: 1 inch = 25.4 mm.

a. As required by Section 502.2.4 and the tabular entry for "Exterior wall *R*-value" shown in Tables 502.2.4(1) through 502.2.4(9), as applicable.

TABLE 502.2.4.16(2)
24-INCH O.C. STEEL-FRAMED WALL EQUIVALENT *R*-VALUES

WOOD-FRAMED WALL *R*-VALUE[a]	EQUIVALENT STEEL-FRAMED WALL CAVITY AND SHEATHING *R*-VALUE
R-11	R-0+R-9, R-11+R-3, R-15+R-2, R-25+R-0
R-13	R-11+R-4, R-15+R-3, R-19+R-2
R-14	R-11+R-5, R-13+R-4, R-15+R-3, R-21+R-2
R-15	R-11+R-5, R-13+R-4, R-19+R-3, R-21+R-2
R-16	R-11+R-7, R-13+R-6, R-19+R-5, R-25+R-4
R-17	R-11+R-8, R-13+R-7, R-15+R-6, R-21+R-5
R-18	R-11+R-8, R-13+R-7, R-19+R-6, R-25+R-5
R-19	R-11+R-19, R-13+R-8, R-15+R-7, R-21+R-6
R-20	R-11+R-9, R-13+R-8, R-19+R-7, R-21+R-6
R-21	R-11+R-9, R-15+R-8, R-21+R-7
R-22	R-11+R-10, R-13+R-9, R-19+R-8, R-21+R-7
R-24	R-11+R-10, R-15+R-9, R-19+R-8
R-25	R-13+R-10, R-19+R-9, R-21+R-8
R-26	R-15+R-10, R-19+R-9, R-25+R-8

For SI: 1 inch = 25.4 mm.

a. As required by Section 502.2.4 and the tabular entry for "Exterior wall *R*-value" shown in Tables 502.2.4(1) through 502.2.4(9), as applicable.

TABLE 502.2.4.17(1) – TABLE 502.2.5   RESIDENTIAL—COMPONENT PERFORMANCE APPROACH

TABLE 502.2.4.17(1)
HIGH-MASS WALL EQUIVALENT R-VALUES
INSULATION PLACED ON THE EXTERIOR OF THE WALL OR WITH INTEGRAL INSULATION

WOOD FRAMED WALL R-VALUE[a]	EQUIVALENT HIGH-MASS WALL R-VALUE					
	HDD 0-1,999	HDD 2,000-3,999	HDD 4,000-5,499	HDD 5,500-6,499	HDD 6,500-8,499	HDD ≥ 8,500
R-11	R-6	R-6	R-7	R-8	R-9	R-10
R-13	R-6	R-6	R-8	R-9	R-10	R-11
R-14	R-6	R-7	R-8	R-9	R-10	R-11
R-15	R-7	R-7	R-8	R-9	R-10	R-12
R-16	R-7	R-7	R-8	R-9	R-11	R-12
R-17	R-7	R-7	R-9	R-10	R-11	R-13
R-18	R-7	R-7	R-9	R-10	R-11	R-13
R-19	R-8	R-9	R-10	R-11	R-13	R-15
R-20	R-8	R-9	R-10	R-11	R-13	R-16
R-21	R-8	R-9	R-10	R-12	R-14	R-16
R-22	R-8	R-9	R-10	R-12	R-14	R-17
R-23	R-9	R-9	R-11	R-12	R-14	R-17
R-24	R-9	R-9	R-11	R-12	R-14	R-17
R-25	R-9	R-10	R-11	R-13	R-15	R-18
R-26	R-9	R-10	R-11	R-13	R-15	R-18

a. As required by Section 502.2.4 and the tabular entry for "Exterior wall R-value" shown in Tables 502.2.4(1) through 502.2.4(9), as applicable.

TABLE 502.2.4.17(2)
HIGH-MASS WALL EQUIVALENT R-VALUES
INSULATION PLACED ON THE INTERIOR OF THE WALL

WOOD FRAMED WALL R-VALUE[a]	EQUIVALENT HIGH-MASS WALL R-VALUE					
	HDD 0-1,999	HDD 2,000-3,999	HDD 4,000-5,499	HDD 5,500-6,499	HDD 6,500-8,499	HDD ≥ 8,500
R-11	R-10	R-10	R-11	R-11	R-12	R-12
R-13	R-11	R-11	R-12	R-12	R-14	R-14
R-14	R-12	R-12	R-12	R-12	R-15	R-15
R-15	R-13	R-13	R-13	R-13	R-15	R-15
R-16	R-13	R-13	R-13	R-14	R-15	R-15
R-17	R-14	R-14	R-14	R-15	R-16	R-16
R-18	R-15	R-15	R-15	R-15	R-16	R-16
R-19	R-16	R-16	R-16	R-19	R-19	R-19
R-20	R-16	R-16	R-16	R-20	R-20	R-20
R-21	R-17	R-17	R-17	R-21	R-21	R-21
R-22	R-17	R-17	R-17	R-21	R-21	R-21
R-23	R-18	R-18	R-18	R-22	R-22	R-22
R-24	R-19	R-19	R-19	R-22	R-22	R-22
R-25	R-20	R-20	R-20	R-22	R-22	R-22
R-26	R-21	R-21	R-21	R-23	R-23	R-23

a. As required by Section 502.2.4 and the tabular entry for "Exterior wall R-value" shown in Tables 502.2.4(1) through 502.2.4(9), as applicable.

TABLE 502.2.5
PRESCRIPTIVE ENVELOPE COMPONENT CRITERIA ADDITIONS TO AND
REPLACEMENT WINDOWS FOR EXISTING DETACHED ONE- AND TWO-FAMILY DWELLINGS

N
Y

HEATING DEGREE DAYS	MAXIMUM	MINIMUM					
	Fenestration U-factor[e]	Ceiling R-value[a]	Wall R-value	Floor R-value	Basement wall R-value[b]	Slab perimeter R-value and depth[c]	Crawl space wall R-value[d]
0-1,999	0.75	R-26	R-13	R-11	R-5	R-0	R-5
2,000-3,999	0.5	R-30	R-13	R-19	R-8	R-5, 2 ft.	R-10
4,000-5,999	0.4	R-38	R-18	R-21	R-10	R-9, 2 ft.	R-19
6,000-8,499	0.35	R-49	R-21	R-21	R-11	R-13, 4 ft.	R-20
8,500-12,999	0.35	R-49	R-21	R-21	R-19	R-18, 4 ft.	R-20

For SI: 1 foot = 304.8 mm.

a. "Ceiling R-value" shall be required for flat or inclined (cathedral) ceilings. Floors over outside air shall meet "Ceiling R-value" requirements.

b. Basement wall insulation shall be installed in accordance with Section 502.2.1.6.

c. Slab perimeter insulation shall be installed in accordance with Section 502.2.1.4. An additional R-2 shall be added to "Slab perimeter R-value" in the table if the slab is heated.

d. "Crawl space wall R-value" shall apply to unventilated crawl spaces only. Crawl space insulation shall be installed in accordance with Section 502.2.1.5.

e. Sunroom additions that maintain thermal isolation shall be required to have a maximum U-factor of 0.50 in locations ≥ 2,000 HDD.

SECTION 503
BUILDING MECHANICAL SYSTEMS
AND EQUIPMENT

503.1 General. This section covers mechanical systems and equipment used to provide heating, ventilating and air-conditioning functions. This section assumes that the residential building and dwelling units therein will be designed with individual HVAC systems. Where equipment not shown in Table 503.2 is specified, it shall meet the provisions of Sections 803.2.2 and 803.3.2.

503.2 Mechanical equipment efficiency. Equipment shown in Table 503.2 shall meet the specified minimum performance. Data furnished by the equipment supplier, or certified under a nationally recognized certification procedure, shall be used to satisfy these requirements. All such equipment shall be installed in accordance with the manufacturer's instructions.

503.3 HVAC systems. HVAC systems shall meet the criteria set forth in Sections 503.3.1 through 503.3.3.

[M] 503.3.1 Load calculations. Heating and cooling system design loads for the purpose of sizing systems and equipment shall be determined in accordance with the procedures described in the ASHRAE *Handbook of Fundamentals* or an equivalent computation procedure, using the design parameters specified in Chapter 3.

503.3.2 Temperature and humidity controls. Temperature and humidity controls shall be provided in accordance with Sections 503.3.2.1 through 503.3.2.4.

503.3.2.1 System controls. Each dwelling unit shall have at least one thermostat capable of automatically adjusting the space temperature set point of the largest zone.

Exception: Radiant floor-heating systems.

Each heating and cooling system shall include at least one temperature control device.

503.3.2.2 Thermostatic control capabilities. Where used to control comfort heating, thermostatic controls shall be capable of being set locally or remotely by adjustment or selection of sensors down to 55°F (13°C) or lower.

Where used to control comfort cooling, thermostatic controls shall be capable of being set locally or remotely by adjustment or selection of sensors up to 85°F (29°C) or higher.

Where used to control both comfort heating and cooling, thermostatic controls shall be capable of providing a temperature range or deadband of at least 5°F (Δ3°C) within which the supply of heating and cooling energy is shut off or reduced to a minimum.

Exception: Thermostats that require manual change-over between heating and cooling modes.

503.3.2.3 Heat pump auxiliary heat. Heat pumps having supplementary electric resistance heaters shall have controls that prevent heater operation when the heating load is capable of being met by the heat pump. Supplemental heater operation is not allowed except during outdoor coil defrost cycles not exceeding 15 minutes.

503.3.2.4 Humidistat. Humidistats used for comfort purposes shall be capable of being set to prevent the use of fossil fuel or electricity to reduce relative humidity below 60 percent or increase relative humidity above 30 percent.

TABLE 503.2
MINIMUM EQUIPMENT PERFORMANCE

EQUIPMENT CATEGORY	SUB-CATEGORY[e]	REFERENCED STANDARD	MINIMUM PERFORMANCE
Air-cooled heat pumps heating mode <65,000 Btu/h cooling capacity	Split systems	ARI 210/240	6.8 HSPF [a,b]
	Single package		6.6 HSPF [a,b]
Gas-fired or oil-fired furnace < 225,000 Btu/h	—	DOE 10 CFR Part 430, Subpart B, Appendix N	AFUE 78%[b] E_t 80%[c]
Gas-fired or oil-fired steam and hot-water boilers < 300,000 Btu/h	—	DOE 10 CFR Part 430, Subpart B, Appendix N	AFUE 80%[b,d]
Air-cooled air conditioners and heat pumps cooling mode < 65,000 Btu/h cooling capacity	Split systems	ARI 210/240	10.0 SEER[b]
	Single package		9.7 SEER[b]

For SI: 1 Btu/h = 0.2931 W.

a. For multicapacity equipment, the minimum performance shall apply to each capacity step provided. Multicapacity refers to manufacturer-published ratings for more than one capacity mode allowed by the product's controls.

b. This is used to be consistent with the National Appliance Energy Conservation Act (NAECA) of 1987 (Public Law 100-12).

c. These requirements apply to combination units not covered by NAECA (three-phase power or cooling capacity 65,000 Btu/h).

d. Except for gas-fired steam boilers for which the minimum AFUE shall be 75 percent.

e. Seasonal rating.

503.3.3 Distribution system, construction and insulation. Distribution systems shall be constructed and insulated in accordance with Sections 503.3.3.1 through 503.3.3.7.

503.3.3.1 Piping insulation. All HVAC system piping shall be thermally insulated in accordance with Table 503.3.3.1.

Exceptions:

1. Factory-installed piping within HVAC equipment tested and rated in accordance with Section 503.2.

2. Piping that conveys fluids which have a design operating temperature range between 55°F and 105°F (13°C and 41°C).

3. Piping that conveys fluids which have not been heated or cooled through the use of fossil fuels or electricity.

4. Heating piping within the building envelope located in detached one- and two-family dwelling units or townhouses.

503.3.3.2 Other insulation thicknesses. Insulation thicknesses in Table 503.3.3.1 are based on insulation having thermal resistivity in the range of 4.0 to 4.6 h · ft² · °F/Btu/inch (0.704 to 0.810 m² · K/W per 25 mm) of thickness on a flat surface at a mean temperature of 75°F (24°C).

Minimum insulation thickness shall be increased for materials having values less than 4.0, or shall be permitted to be reduced for materials having thermal resistivity values greater than 4.6 in accordance with Equation 5-9.

$$\frac{4.6 \times \text{Table 503.3.3.1 Thickness}}{\text{Actual Resistivity}} = \begin{array}{l}\text{New}\\\text{Minimum}\\\text{Thickness}\end{array}$$

(Equation 5-9)

For materials with thermal resistivity values less than 4.0, the minimum insulation thickness shall be permitted to be increased in accordance with Equation 5-10.

$$\frac{4.0 \times \text{Table 503.3.3.1 Thickness}}{\text{Actual Resistivity}} = \begin{array}{l}\text{New}\\\text{Minimum}\\\text{Thickness}\end{array}$$

(Equation 5-10)

503.3.3.3 Duct and plenum insulation. All supply and return-air ducts and plenums installed as part of an HVAC air-distribution system shall be thermally insulated in accordance with Table 503.3.3.3, or where such ducts or plenums operate at static pressures greater than 2 in. w.g. (500 Pa), in accordance with Section 503.3.3.4.1.

Exceptions:

1. Factory-installed plenums, casings or ductwork furnished as a part of the HVAC equipment tested and rated in accordance with Section 503.2.

2. Ducts within the building envelope located in detached one- and two-family dwellings and townhouses.

[M] 503.3.3.4 Duct construction. Ductwork shall be constructed and erected in accordance with the *Mechanical Code of New York State.*

TABLE 503.3.3.1
MINIMUM PIPE INSULATION
(thickness in inches)

PIPING SYSTEM TYPES	FLUID TEMPERATURE RANGE, °F	PIPE SIZES[a]					
		Runouts up to 2″[b]	1 and less	1.25″ to 2″	2.5″ to 4″	5″ to 6″	8″ and larger
HEATING SYSTEMS							
Steam and hot water:							
High pressure/temperature	306-450	1$^1/_2$	2$^1/_2$	2$^1/_2$	3	3$^1/_2$	3$^1/_2$
Medium pressure/temperature	251-305	1$^1/_2$	2	2$^1/_2$	2$^1/_2$	3	3
Low pressure/temperature	201-250	1	1$^1/_2$	1$^1/_2$	2	2	2
Low temperature	106-200	$^1/_2$	1	1	1$^1/_2$	1$^1/_2$	1$^1/_2$
Steam condensate (for feed water)	Any	1	1	1$^1/_2$	2	2	2
COOLING SYSTEMS							
Chilled water, refrigerant and brine:	40-55	$^1/_2$	$^1/_2$	$^3/_4$	1	1	1
	Below 40	1	1	1$^1/_2$	1$^1/_2$	1$^1/_2$	1$^1/_2$

For SI: 1 inch = 25.4 mm, 1 foot = 304.8 mm, °C = [(°F)-32]/1.8.

a. For piping exposed to outdoor air, increase insulation thickness by 0.5 inch.

b. Runouts not exceeding 12 feet in length to individual terminal units.

503.3.3.4.1 High- and medium-pressure duct systems. All ducts and plenums operating at static pressures greater than 2 in. w.g. (500 Pa) shall be insulated and sealed in accordance with Section 803.2.8. Ducts operating at static pressures in excess of 3 in. w.g. (750 Pa) shall be leak tested in accordance with Section 803.3.6. Pressure classifications specific to the duct system shall be clearly indicated on the construction documents in accordance with the *Mechanical Code of New York State.*

503.3.3.4.2 Low-pressure duct systems. All longitudinal and transverse joints, seams and connections of supply and return ducts operating at static pressures less than or equal to 2 in. w.g. (500 Pa) shall be securely fastened and sealed with welds, gaskets, mastics (adhesives), masti-plus-embedded-fabric systems or tapes installed in accordance with the manufacturer's installation instructions. Pressure classifications specific to the duct system shall be clearly indicated on the construction documents in accordance with the *Mechanical Code of New York State.*

Exception: Continuously welded and locking-type longitudinal joints and seams on ducts operating at static pressures less than 2 in. w.g. (500 Pa) pressure classification.

503.3.3.4.3 Sealing required. All joints, longitudinal and transverse seams, and connections in ductwork shall be securely fastened and sealed with welds, gaskets, mastics (adhesives), mastic-plus-embedded-fabric systems or tapes. Tapes and mastics used to seal ductwork shall be listed and labeled in accordance with UL 181A or UL 181B. Duct connections to flanges of air distribution system equipment shall be sealed and mechanically fastened. Unlisted duct tape is not permitted as a sealant on any metal ducts.

503.3.3.5 Mechanical ventilation. Each mechanical ventilation system (supply or exhaust, or both) shall be equipped with a readily accessible switch or other means for shutoff, or volume reduction and shutoff, when ventilation is not required. Automatic or gravity dampers that close when the system is not operating shall be provided for outdoor air intakes and exhausts.

503.3.3.6 Transport energy. The air-transport factor for each all-air system shall be not less than 5.5 when calculated in accordance with Equation 5-11. Energy for transfer of air through heat-recovery devices shall not be included in determining the air transport factor.

$$\text{Transport Factor} = \frac{\text{Space Sensible Heat Removal}^a}{\text{Supply + Return Fan(s) Power Input}^a}$$

(Equation 5-11)

a. Expressed in consistent units either Btu/h or watts.

For purposes of these calculations, space sensible heat removal is equivalent to the maximum coincident design sensible cooling load of all spaces served for which the system provides cooling. Fan power input is the rate of energy delivered to the fan prime mover.

Air and water, all-water and unitary systems employing chilled, hot, dual-temperature or condenser water-transport systems to space terminals shall not require greater transport energy (including central and terminal fan power and pump power) than an equivalent all-air system providing the same space sensible heat removal and having an air-transport factor of not less than 5.5.

TABLE 503.3.3.3
MINIMUM DUCT INSULATION[a]

ANNUAL HEATING DEGREE DAYS	Insulation R-value (h·ft^2·°F)/Btu[d]			
	Ducts in unconditioned attics or outside building		Ducts in unconditioned basements, crawl spaces, garages, and other unconditioned spaces[c]	
	Supply	Return	Supply	Return[b]
Below 1,500	8	4	4	0
1,500 to 3,500	8	4	6	2
3,501 to 7,500	8	4	8	2
Above 7,500	11	6	11	2

For SI: °C= [(°F)-32]/1.8, 1 (h·ft^2·°F)/Btu = 0.176(m^2·K)/W, 1 foot = 304.8 mm.

a. Insulation R-values shown are for the insulation as installed and do not include film resistance. The required minimum R-values do not consider water vapor transmission and condensation. Where control of condensation is required, additional insulation, vapor retarders, or both, shall be provided to limit vapor transmission and condensation. For ducts that are designed to convey both heated and cooled air, duct insulation shall be as required by the most restrictive condition. Where exterior walls are used as plenums, wall insulation shall be as required by the most restrictive condition of this section.

b. Insulation on return ducts in basements is not required.

c. Unconditioned spaces include ventilated crawl spaces, ventilated attics, and framed cavities in those floor, wall and ceiling assemblies which (1) separate conditioned space from unconditioned space or outside air, and (2) are uninsulated on the side facing away from the conditioned space.

d. Insulation resistance measured on a horizontal plane in accordance with ASTM C 518, at a mean temperature of 75°F.

503.3.3.7 Balancing. The HVAC system design shall provide means for balancing air and water systems. Balancing mechanisms shall include, but not be limited to, dampers, temperature and pressure test connections, and balancing valves.

SECTION 504
SERVICE WATER HEATING

504.1 Scope. The purpose of this section is to provide criteria for design and equipment selection that will produce energy savings when applied to service water heating. Water supplies to ice-making machines and refrigerators shall be taken from a cold-water line of the water distribution system.

504.2 Water heaters, storage tanks and boilers. Water heaters, storage tanks and boilers shall meet the performance criteria set forth in Sections 504.2.1 and 504.2.2.

504.2.1 Performance efficiency. Water heaters and hot water storage tanks shall meet the minimum performance of water-heating equipment specified in Table 504.2. Where multiple criteria are listed, all criteria shall be met.

Exception: Storage water heaters and hot water storage tanks having more than 140 gallons (530 L) of storage capacity need not meet the standby loss (*SL*) or heat loss (*HL*) requirements of Table 504.2 if the tank surface area is thermally insulated to R-12.5 and if a standing pilot light is not used.

504.2.2 Combination service water-heating/space-heating boilers. Service water-heating equipment shall not be dependent on year-round operation of space-heating boilers; that is, boilers that have as another function winter space heating.

Exceptions:

1. Systems with service/space-heating boilers having a standby loss (Btu/h) (W) less than:

$$\frac{13.3 \, pmd}{n} \qquad \text{(Equation 5-12)}$$

determined by the fixture count method where:

pmd = Probable maximum demand in gallons/hour as determined in accordance with Chapter 37 of the ASHRAE *HVAC Systems and Applications Handbook*.

n = Fraction of year when outdoor daily mean temperature exceeds 64.9°F (18°C).

The standby loss is to be determined for a test period of 24-hour duration while maintaining a boiler water temperature of 90°F (32.2°C) above an ambient of 60 to 90°F (16 to 32°C) and a 5-foot (1524 mm) stack on appliance.

2. For systems where the use of a single heating unit will lead to energy savings, such unit shall be utilized.

504.3 Swimming pools. Swimming pools shall be provided with energy-conserving measures in accordance with Sections 504.3.1 through 504.3.3.

504.3.1 On-off switch. All pool heaters shall be equipped with an ON-OFF switch mounted for easy access to allow shutting off the operation of the heater without adjusting the thermostat setting and to allow restarting without relighting the pilot light.

504.3.2 Pool covers. Heated swimming pools shall be equipped with a pool cover.

Exception: Outdoor pools deriving over 20 percent of the energy for heating from renewable sources (computed over an operating season) are exempt from this requirement.

504.3.3 Time clocks. Time clocks shall be installed so that the pump can be set to run in the off-peak electric demand period and can be set for the minimum time necessary to maintain the water in a clear and sanitary condition in keeping with applicable health standards.

504.4 Pump operation. Circulating hot water systems shall be arranged so that the circulation pump(s) can be conveniently turned off, automatically or manually, when the hot water system is not in operation.

504.5 Pipe insulation. For recirculating systems, piping heat loss shall be limited to a maximum of 17.5 Btu/h per linear foot (16.8 W/m) of pipe in accordance with Table 504.5, which is based on design external temperature no lower than 65°F (18°C). Other design temperatures must be calculated.

Exception: Piping insulation is not required when the heat loss of the piping, without insulation, does not increase the annual energy requirements of the building.

504.6 Conservation of hot water. Hot water shall be conserved in accordance with Section 504.6.1.

504.6.1 Showers. Shower heads shall have a maximum flow rate of 2.5 gallons per minute (gpm) (0.158 L/s) at a pressure of 80 pounds per square inch (psi) (551 kPa) when tested in accordance with ASME A112.18.1.

TABLE 504.2
MINIMUM PERFORMANCE OF WATER-HEATING EQUIPMENT

CATEGORY	TYPE	FUEL	INPUT RATING	V_T[a] (gallons)	INPUT TO V_T RATIO (Btuh/gal)	TEST METHOD	ENERGY FACTOR[b]	THERMAL EFFICIENCY E_t (percent)	STANDBY LOSS (percent/hour) [a]
NAECA-covered water-heating equipment[c]	All	Electric	≤ 12kW	All[e]	—	Note f	≥ 0.93-0.00132V*	—	—
	Storage	Gas	≤ 75,000 Btu/h	All[e]	—	Note f	≥ 0.62-0.0019V*	—	—
	Instantaneous	Gas	≤ 200,000 Btu/h[e]	All	—	Note f	≥ 0.62-0.0019V*	—	—
	Storage	Oil	≤ 105,000 Btu/h	All	—	Note f	≥ 0.59-0.0019V*	—	—
	Instantaneous	Oil	≤ 210,000 Btu/h	All	—	Note f	≥ 0.59-0.0019V*	—	—
	Pool heater	Gas/oil	All	All	—	Note g	—	≥ 78%	—
Other water-heating equipment[d]	Storage	Electric	All	All	—	Note h	—	—	≤ 0.30+27/V_T*
	Storage/ instantaneous	Gas/oil	≤ 155,000 Btu/h	All	< 4,000	Note h	—	≥ 78%	≤ 1.3+114/V_T*
			> 155,000 Btu/h	All	< 4,000	Note h	—	≥ 78%	≤ 1.3+95/V_T*
				< 10 ≥ 10	≥ 4,000 ≥ 4,000	Note h	—	≥ 80% ≥ 77%	≤ 2.3+67/V_T*
Unfired storage tanks	—	—	—	All	—	—	—	—	≤ 6.5Btuh/ft^{2i}*

For SI: 1 Btu/ft^2 = 3.155 W/m^2, 1 Btu/h = 0.2931 W, 1 gallon = 3.785 L, °C = [(°F)-32]/1.8.

a. V_T is the storage volume in gallons as measured during the standby loss test. For the purpose of estimating the standby loss requirement using the rated volume shown on the rating plate, V_T should be no less than 0.95V for gas and oil water heaters and no less than 0.90V for electric water heaters.

b. V is rated storage volume in gallons as specified by the manufacturer.

c. Consistent with National Appliance Energy Conservation Act (NAECA) of 1987.

d. All except those water heaters covered by NAECA.

e. DOE 10 CFR; Part 430, Subpart B, Appendix E applies to electric and gas storage water heaters with rated volumes 20 gallons and gas instantaneous water heaters with input ratings of 50,000 to 200,000 Btu/h.

f. DOE 10 CFR; Part 430, Subpart B, Appendix E.

g. ANSI Z21.56.

h. ANSI Z21.10.3. When testing an electric storage water heater for standby loss using the test procedure of Section 2.9 of ANSI Z21.10.3, the electrical supply voltage shall be maintained within ± 1 percent of the center of the voltage range specified on the water heater nameplate. Also, when needed for calculations, the thermal efficiency (E_t) shall be 98 percent. When testing an oil water heater using the test procedures of Sections 2.8 and 2.9 of ANSI Z21.10.3, the following modifications will be made: A vertical length of the flue pipe shall be connected to the flue gas outlet of sufficient height to establish the minimum draft specified in the manufacturer's installation instructions. All measurements of oil consumption will be taken by instruments with an accuracy of ±1 percent or better. The burner shall be adjusted to achieve an hourly Btu input rate within ± 2 percent of the manufacturer's specified input rate with the CO_2 reading as specified by the manufacturer with smoke no greater than 1 and the fuel pump pressure within ± 1 percent of the manufacturer's specification.

i. Heat loss of tank surface area (Btu/h · ft^2) based on 80°F water-air temperature difference.

* Minimum efficiencies marked with an asterisk are established by preemptive federal law and are printed for the convenience of the user.

TABLE 504.5
MINIMUM PIPE INSULATION
(thickness in inches)

SERVICE WATER-HEATING TEMPERATURES °F	PIPE SIZES[a]			
	Noncirculating runouts	Circulating mains and runouts		
	Up to 1"	Up to 1.25"	1.50" to 2"	Over 2"
170-180	0.5	1.0	1.5	2.0
140-169	0.5	0.5	1.0	1.5
100-139	0.5	0.5	0.5	1.0

For SI: 1 inch = 25.4 mm, °C = [(°F)-32]/1.8,
    1 Btu/h/inch · ft^2 · °F = 0.144 W/(m · K).

a. Nominal iron pipe size and insulation thickness. Conductivity, $k \cong 0.27$

504.7 Heat traps. Water heaters with vertical pipe risers shall have a heat trap on both the inlet and outlet of the water heater unless the water heater has an integral heat trap or is part of a circulating system.

SECTION 505
ELECTRICAL POWER AND LIGHTING

505.1 Electrical energy consumption. See Section 102.6. NY

505.2 Lighting power budget. The lighting system shall meet the applicable provisions of Section 805.

Exception: Detached one- and two-family dwellings and NY townhouses, and the dwelling portion of Type R-2 and R-4 NY residential buildings.

CHAPTER 6

SIMPLIFIED PRESCRIPTIVE REQUIREMENTS FOR <u>DETACHED</u> ONE- AND TWO-FAMILY DWELLINGS AND TYPE R-2, R-4 OR <u>TOWNHOUSE</u> RESIDENTIAL BUILDINGS

SECTION 601
GENERAL

601.1 Scope. This chapter sets forth energy-efficiency-related requirements for the design and construction of <u>detached one-</u> <u>and two-family dwellings</u> and <u>R-2, R-4 and townhouse</u> residential buildings.

Exception: Portions of the building envelope that do not enclose conditioned space.

601.2 Compliance. Compliance shall be demonstrated in accordance with Section 601.2.1 or 601.2.2.

601.2.1 Residential buildings, <u>detached one- and two-</u> <u>family dwellings</u>. Compliance for <u>detached one- and two-</u> <u>family dwellings</u> shall be demonstrated by either:

1. Meeting the requirements of this chapter for buildings with a glazing area that does not exceed 15 percent of the gross area of exterior walls; or

2. Meeting the requirements of Chapter 4 or Chapter 5 for <u>detached one- and two-family dwellings</u>.

601.2.2 Residential buildings, Type <u>R-2, R-4 or town-</u> <u>house.</u> Compliance for Type <u>R-2, R-4 or townhouse</u> residential buildings shall be demonstrated by either:

1. Meeting the requirements of this chapter for buildings with a glazing area that does not exceed 25 percent of the gross area of exterior walls; or

2. Meeting the requirements of Chapter 4 or Chapter 5 for Type <u>R-2, R-4 or townhouse</u> residential buildings.

601.3 Materials and equipment. Materials and equipment shall be identified in a manner that will allow a determination of their compliance with the applicable provisions of this chapter. Materials and equipment used to conform to the applicable provisions of this chapter shall be installed in accordance with the manufacturer's installation instructions.

601.3.1 Insulation. The thermal resistance (*R*-value) shall be indicated on all insulation and the insulation installed such that the *R*-value can be verified during inspection, or a certification of the installed *R*-value shall be provided at the job site by the insulation installer. Where blown-in or sprayed insulation is applied in walls, the installer shall provide a certification of the installed density and *R*-value. Where blown-in or sprayed insulation is applied in the roof/ceiling assembly, the installer shall provide a certification of the initial installed thickness, settled thickness, coverage area, and number of bags of insulating material installed. Markers shall be provided for every 300 square feet (28 m^2) of area, attached to the trusses, rafters, or joists, and indicate in 1-inch-high (25 mm) numbers the installed thickness of the insulation.

601.3.1.1 Moisture control. The design shall not create conditions of accelerated deterioration from moisture condensation. Frame walls and floors shall be provided with an approved vapor retarder having a maximum permeance rating of 1.0 perm (5.72 × 10^{-8}g/Pa · s · m^2) when tested in accordance with Procedure A of ASTM E 96. The vapor retarder shall be installed on the warm-in-winter side of the thermal insulation.

Exceptions:

1. In construction where moisture or its freezing will not damage the materials.

2. Where other approved means to avoid condensation in unventilated framed wall, floor, roof and ceiling cavities are provided.

601.3.2 Fenestration. The *U*-factor of fenestration shall be determined in accordance with NFRC 100 by an accredited, independent laboratory, and labeled and certified by the manufacturer. The solar heat gain coefficient (SHGC) of fenestration shall be determined in accordance with NFRC 200 by an accredited, independent laboratory, and labeled and certified by the manufacturer.

601.3.2.1 Default fenestration performance. Where a manufacturer has not determined a fenestration product's *U*-factor in accordance with NFRC 100, compliance shall be determined by assigning such products a default *U*-factor from Tables 102.5.2(1) and 102.5.2(2). When a manufacturer has not determined a fenestration product's SHGC in accordance with NFRC 200, compliance shall be determined by assigning such products a default SHGC from Table 102.5.2(3).

601.3.2.2 Air leakage. The air leakage of prefabricated fenestration shall be determined in accordance with AAMA/WDMA 101/I.S.2 by an accredited independent laboratory, and labeled and certified by the manufacturer. Alternatively, the manufacturer shall certify that the fenestration is installed in accordance with Section 502.1.4.

601.3.3 Maintenance. Where mechanical or plumbing system components require preventive maintenance for efficient operation, regular maintenance requirements shall be clearly stated and affixed to the component, or the source for such information shall be shown on a label attached to the component.

TABLE 602.1(1) – 602.1.1.1   SIMPLIFIED PRESCRIPTIVE REQUIREMENTS

TABLE 602.1(1)
SIMPLIFIED PRESCRIPTIVE BUILDING ENVELOPE THERMAL COMPONENT CRITERIA
MINIMUM REQUIRED THERMAL PERFORMANCE (*U*-FACTOR AND *R*-VALUE)

HEATING DEGREE DAYS	Maximum	Minimum					
	Glazing *U*-factor	Ceiling *R*-value	Wall *R*-value	Floor *R*-value	Basement wall *R*-value	Slab perimeter *R*-value and depth	Crawl space wall *R*-value
0-499	Any	R-13	R-11	R-11	R-0	R-0	R-0
500-999	0.90	R-19	R-11	R-11	R-0	R-0	R-4
1,000-1,499	0.75	R-19	R-11	R-11	R-0	R-0	R-5
1,500-1,999	0.75	R-26	R-13	R-11	R-5	R-0	R-5
2,000-2,499	0.65	R-30	R-13	R-11	R-5	R-0	R-6
2,500-2,999	0.60	R-30	R-13	R-19	R-6	R-4, 2 ft.	R-7
3,000-3,400	0.55	R-30	R-13	R-19	R-7	R-4, 2 ft.	R-8
3,500-3,999	0.50	R-30	R-13	R-19	R-8	R-5, 2 ft.	R-10
4,000-4,499	0.45	R-38	R-13	R-19	R-8	R-5, 2 ft.	R-11
4,500-4,999	0.45	R-38	R-16	R-19	R-9	R-6, 2 ft.	R-17
5,000-5,499	0.45	R-38	R-18	R-19	R-9	R-6, 2 ft.	R-17
5,500-5,999	0.40	R-38	R-18	R-21	R-10	R-9, 4 ft.	R-19
6,000-6,499	0.35	R-38	R-18	R-21	R-10	R-9, 4 ft.	R-20
6,500-6,999	0.35	R-49	R-21	R-21	R-11	R-11, 4 ft.	R-20
7,000-8,499	0.35	R-49	R-21	R-21	R-11	R-13, 4 ft.	R-20
8,500-8,999	0.35	R-49	R-21	R-21	R-18	R-14, 4 ft.	R-20
9,000-12,999	0.35	R-49	R-21	R-21	R-19	R-18, 4 ft.	R-20

For SI: 1 foot = 304.8 mm.

601.3.4 Recessed lighting fixtures. When installed in the building envelope, recessed lighting fixtures shall meet one of the following requirements:

1. Type IC rated, manufactured with no penetrations between the inside of the recessed fixture and ceiling cavity, and sealed or gasketed to prevent air leakage into the unconditioned space.

2. Type IC or non-IC rated, installed inside a sealed box constructed from a minimum 0.5-inch-thick (12.7 mm) gypsum wallboard or constructed from a preformed polymeric vapor barrier, or other air-tight assembly manufactured for this purpose, while maintaining required clearance of not less than 0.5 inch (12.7 mm) from combustible material and not less than 3 inches (76 mm) from insulation material.

3. Type IC rated, in accordance with ASTM E 283 no more than 2.0 cubic feet per minute (cfm) (0.944 L/s) air movement from the conditioned space to the ceiling cavity. The lighting fixture shall be tested at 1.57 psi (75 Pa) pressure difference and shall be labeled.

SECTION 602
BUILDING ENVELOPE

602.1 Thermal performance criteria. The minimum required insulation *R*-value or maximum required *U*-factor for each element in the building thermal envelope (fenestration, roof/ceiling, opaque wall, floor, slab edge, crawl space wall and basement wall) shall be in accordance with the criteria in Table 602.1(1) or Table 602.1(2) for electric resistance heating.

Detached one- and two-family dwellings, with greater than 15-percent glazing area; Type R-2, R-4 or townhouse residential buildings, with greater than 25-percent glazing area; and any residential buildings in climates with heating degree days (HDD) equal to or greater than 13,000; shall determine compliance using the building envelope requirements of Chapter 4 or Chapter 5.

602.1.1 Exterior walls. The sum of the *R*-values of the insulation materials installed in framing cavities and insulating sheathing (where used) shall meet or exceed the minimum required "Wall *R*-value" in Table 602.1(1). Framing, drywall, structural sheathing, or exterior siding materials shall not be considered contributing, in any way, to the thermal performance of exterior walls. Insulation separated from the conditioned space by a vented space shall not be counted towards the required *R*-value.

602.1.1.1 Mass walls. Mass walls shall be permitted to meet the criteria in Table 602.1.1.1(1) based on the insulation position and the climate zone where the building is located. Other mass walls shall meet the frame wall criteria for the building type and the climate zone where the building is located, based on the sum of interior and exterior insulation. Walls with "exterior insulation" position have the entire effective mass layer interior to an insulation layer. Walls with "integral insulation" position have either insulation and mass materials well mixed as in wood (logs); or substantially equal amounts of mass material on the interior and exterior of insulation as in concrete masonry units with insulated cores or masonry cavity walls. Walls with interior insulation position have the mass material located exterior to the insulating material(s). Walls not meeting the above descriptions for exterior or integral positions shall meet the requirements for "other mass walls" in Table 602.1.1.1(1). The *R*-value of the mass assembly for typical masonry construction shall be taken from Table 602.1.1.1(2). The mass assembly *R*-value for a solid concrete wall with a thickness of 4 inches or greater is R-1.1. *R*-values for other assemblies are permitted to be based on the hot box tests referenced in ASTM C 236 or ASTM C 976, two-dimensional calculations or isothermal plane calculations.

602.1.1.2 Steel-frame walls. The minimum required *R*-values for steel-frame walls shall be in accordance with Table 602.1.1.2.

TABLE 602.1.1.2
STEEL-FRAME WALL MINIMUM
PERFORMANCE REQUIREMENTS (*R*-VALUE)

HDD	EQUIVALENT STEEL-FRAME WALL CAVITY AND SHEATHING *R*-VALUE[a]
0-1,999	R-11+R-5, R-15+R-4, R-21+R-3
2,000-3,999	R-11+R-5, R-15+R-4, R-21+R-3
4,000-5,999	R-11+R-9, R-15+R-8, R-21+R-7
6,000-8,499	R-13+R-10, R-19+R-9, R-25+R-8
8,500-12,999	R-13+R-10, R-19+R-9, R-25+R-8

a. The cavity insulation *R*-value requirement is listed first, followed by the sheathing *R*-value requirement.

602.1.2 Ceilings. The required "Ceiling *R*-value" in Table 602.1(1) assumes standard truss or rafter construction and shall apply to all roof/ceiling portions of the building thermal envelope, including cathedral ceilings. Where the construction technique allows the required *R*-value of ceiling insulation to be obtained over the exterior wall top plate, R-30 shall be permitted to be used where R-38 is required in the table, and R-38 shall be permitted to be used where R-49 is required.

TABLE 602.1(2)
ENVELOPE INSULATION *R*-VALUES AND GLAZING *U*-FACTOR
REQUIREMENTS FOR RESIDENCES USING ELECTRIC
RESISTANCE HEATING

Building Element	Single and Multi-family Houses
Roof/ceiling	R-49
Wall (above grade)[b]	R-26
Glazing *U*-factor[a]	0.31
Floor over unheated space	R-30
Basement wall	R-19, 7 ft. or to top of slab
Slab edge	R-15, 4 ft.

a. Maximum Allowable Glazing: 15% of the wall area.
b. Opaque doors shall have a maximum *U*-factor of 0.35.

602.1.3 Opaque doors. Opaque doors in the building envelope shall have a maximum *U*-factor of 0.35. One opaque door <u>may</u> be exempt from this *U*-factor requirement.

602.1.4 Floor. The required *R*-value in Table 602.1(1) shall apply to all floors, except any individual floor assembly with over 25 percent of its conditioned floor area exposed directly to outside air shall meet the *R*-value requirement in Table 602.1(1) for "Ceiling *R*-value."

602.1.5 Basement walls. Where the basement is considered a conditioned space, the basement walls shall be insulated in accordance with Table 602.1(1). Where the basement is not considered a conditioned space, either the basement wall or the ceiling(s) separating the basement from conditioned space shall be insulated in accordance with Table 602.1.(1) Where basement walls are required to be insulated, the required *R*-value shall be applied from the top of the basement wall to a depth below grade <u>as specified in Table 602.1.5</u> or to the top of the basement floor, whichever is less.

TABLE 602.1.5
FOUNDATION INSULATION DEPTH

Heating Degree Days	Depth Below Grade
Less than or equal to 5000	24″
5001 - 6000	24″
6001 - 7000	48″
7001 - 8000	48″
8001 - 9000	84″

602.1.6 Slab-on-grade floors. For slabs with a top edge 12 inches (305 mm) or less below finished grade, the required "Slab perimeter *R*-value and depth" in Table 602.1(1) shall be applied to the outside of the foundation or the inside of the foundation wall. The insulation shall extend downward from the top of the slab or downward from the top of the slab to the bottom of the slab and then horizontally to the interior or exterior, until the distance listed in Table 602.1(1) is reached.

Where installed between the exterior wall and the edge of the interior slab, the top edge of the insulation shall be permitted to be cut at a 45-degree (0.79 rad) angle away from the exterior wall. Insulation extending horizontally outside of the foundation shall be protected by pavement or by a minimum of 10 inches (254 mm) of soil.

In locations of 500 HDD or greater, R-2 shall be added to the "Slab perimeter *R*-value" in Table 602.1(1) where uninsulated hot water pipes, air distribution ducts, or electric heating cables are installed within or under the slab.

TABLE 602.1.1.1(1) – TABLE 602.1.1.1(2)   SIMPLIFIED PRESCRIPTIVE REQUIREMENTS

TABLE 602.1.1.1(1)
MASS WALL PRESCRIPTIVE BUILDING ENVELOPE REQUIREMENTS

MASS WALL ASSEMBLY R-VALUE[a]			
Building Location		Exterior or Integral Insulation	Other Mass Walls
Zone[b]	HDD	Residential Buildings	Residential Buildings
1	0-499	R-3.8	R-9.7
2	500-999	R-4.8	R-9.7
3	1,000-1,499	R-4.8	R-9.7
4	1,500-1,999	R-8.1	R-10.8
5	2,000-2,499	R-8.9	R-10.8
6	2,500-2,999	R-8.9	R-10.8
7	3,000-3,499	R-8.9	R-10.8
8	3,500-3,999	R-8.9	R-10.8
9	4,000-4,499	R-8.9	R-10.9
10	4,500-4,999	R-10.4	R-12.3
11	5,000-5,499	R-11.9	R-15.2
12	5,500-5,999	R-11.9	R-15.2
13	6,000-6,499	R-11.9	R-15.2
14	6,500-6,999	R-15.5	R-18.4
15	7,000-8,499	R-15.5	R-18.4
16	8,500-8,999	R-18.4	R-18.4
17	9,000-12,999	R-18.4	R-18.4

a. The sum of the value in Table 602.1.1.1(2) and additional insulation layers.
b. This table does not use zone subsets of A or B.

TABLE 602.1.1.1(2)
MASS ASSEMBLY R-VALUES

ASSEMBLY TYPE	UNGROUTED CELLS, NOT INSULATED	UNGROUTED CELLS INSULATED		
		No grout	Vertical cells grouted at 10' O.C. or greater	Vertical cells grouted at less than 10' O.C.
6″ Lightweight concrete block	2.3	5.0	4.5	3.8
6″ Medium-weight concrete block	2.1	4.2	3.8	3.2
6″ Normal-weight concrete block	1.9	3.3	3.1	2.7
8″ Lightweight concrete block	2.6	6.7	5.9	4.8
8″ Medium-weight concrete block	2.3	5.3	4.8	4.0
8″ Normal-weight concrete block	2.1	4.2	3.8	3.3
12″ Lightweight concrete block	2.9	9.1	7.9	6.3
12″ Medium-weight concrete block	2.6	7.1	6.4	5.2
12″ Normal-weight concrete block	2.3	5.6	5.1	4.3
Brick cavity wall	3.7	6.7	6.2	5.4
Hollow clay brick	2.0	2.7	2.6	2.4

For SI: 1 inch = 25.4 mm, 1 foot = 304.8 mm.

602.1.7 Crawl space walls. Where the floor above the crawl space is uninsulated, insulation shall be installed on crawl space walls when the crawl space is not vented to outside air. The required "Crawl space wall R-value" in Table 602.1(1) shall be applied inside of the crawl space wall, downward from the sill plate to the exterior finished grade level and then vertically or horizontally or both for 24 inches (610 mm). The exposed earth in all crawl space foundations shall be covered with a continuous vapor retarder having a maximum permeance rating of 1.0 perm (5.72×10^{-8}g/Pa $\cdot$ s $\cdot$ m^2), when tested in accordance with ASTM E 96.

602.1.8 Masonry veneer. For exterior foundation insulation, the horizontal portion of the foundation which supports a masonry veneer is not required to be insulated.

602.1.9 Protection. Exposed insulating materials applied to the exterior of foundation walls shall have a rigid, opaque and weather-resistant protective covering. The protective covering shall extend 6 inches (152 mm) below finished grade level.

602.1.10 Caulking, sealants and gasketing. All joints, seams, penetrations (site-built windows, doors, and skylights), openings between window and door assemblies and their respective jambs and framing, and other sources of air leakage (infiltration and exfiltration) through the building envelope shall be caulked, gasketed, weatherstripped, wrapped, or otherwise sealed to limit uncontrolled air movement.

602.2 Maximum solar heat gain coefficient for fenestration products. In locations with heating degree days (HDD) less than 3,500, the area-weighted-average solar heat gain coefficient (SHGC) for glazed fenestration installed in the building envelope shall not exceed 0.40.

602.3 Fenestration exemption. Up to 1 percent of the total glazing area <u>may</u> be exempt from the "Glazing U-factor" requirement in Table 602.1(1).

N
Y

602.4 Replacement fenestration. Where an entire fenestration product, including frame, sash, and glazed portion, is being replaced, the replacement fenestration product shall have a U-factor that does not exceed the "Fenestration U-factor" requirement in Table 502.2.5 applicable to the climate zone (HDD) where the building is located. The replacement fenestration product(s) must also satisfy the air leakage requirements and SHGC of Sections 601.3.2.2 and 602.2, respectively.

> **Exception:** Replacement skylights shall have a maximum U-factor of 0.50 when installed in any location above 1,999 HDD.

SECTION 603
MECHANICAL SYSTEMS

603.1 Heating and air-conditioning equipment and appliances. Heating and air-conditioning equipment and appliances shall comply with the applicable requirements of Section 503.

SECTION 604
SERVICE WATER HEATING

604.1 Water-heating equipment and appliances. Water-heating equipment and appliances shall comply with the applicable requirements of Section 504.

CHAPTER 7

BUILDING DESIGN FOR ALL COMMERCIAL BUILDINGS

SECTION 701
SCOPE

701.1 General. Commercial buildings shall meet the requirements of ASHRAE/IESNA 90.1.

Exception: Commercial buildings that comply with Chapter 8.

CHAPTER 8

DESIGN BY ACCEPTABLE PRACTICE
FOR COMMERCIAL BUILDINGS

SECTION 801
SCOPE

801.1 General. The requirements contained in this chapter are applicable to commercial buildings, or portions of commercial buildings. Buildings constructed in accordance with this chapter are deemed to comply with this code.

801.2 Application. The requirements in Sections 802, 803, 804, and 805 shall each be satisfied on an individual basis. Where one or more of these sections is not satisfied, compliance for that section(s) shall be demonstrated in accordance with the applicable provisions of ASHRAE/IESNA 90.1.

SECTION 802
BUILDING ENVELOPE REQUIREMENTS

802.1 General. Walls, roof assemblies, floors, glazing, and slabs on grade which are part of the building envelope for buildings where window and glazed door area is not greater than 50 percent of the gross area of above-grade walls shall meet the requirements of Sections 802.2.1 through 802.2.9, as applicable. Buildings with more glazing shall meet the applicable provisions of ASHRAE/IESNA 90.1.

802.1.1 Classification of walls. Walls associated with the building envelope shall be classified in accordance with Section 802.1.1.1, 802.1.1.2 or 802.1.1.3.

802.1.1.1 Above-grade walls. Above-grade walls are those walls covered by Section 802.2.1 on the exterior of the building and completely above grade or the above-grade portion of a basement or first-story wall that is more than 15 percent above grade.

802.1.1.2 Below-grade walls. Below-grade walls covered by Section 802.2.8 are basement or first-story walls associated with the exterior of the building that are at least 85 percent below grade.

802.1.1.3 Interior walls. Interior walls covered by Section 802.2.9 are those walls not on the exterior of the building and that separate conditioned and unconditioned space.

802.1.2 Moisture control. All framed walls, floors and ceilings not ventilated to allow moisture to escape shall be provided with an approved vapor retarder having a maximum permeance rating of 1.0 perm $(5.72 \times 10^{-8} \, g/Pa \cdot s \cdot m^2)$, when tested in accordance with Procedure A of ASTM E 96, on the warm-in-winter side of the insulation.

Exceptions:

1. Buildings located in Climate Zones 1 through 7 as indicated in Table 302.1.

2. In construction where moisture or its freezing will not damage the materials.

3. Where other approved means to avoid condensation in unventilated frame wall, floor, roof and ceiling cavities are provided.

802.2 Criteria. The building envelope components shall meet each of the applicable requirements in Tables 802.2(1) through 802.2(7)[beginning on page 78], based on the percentage of wall that is glazed and on climate zone. The percentage of wall that is glazed shall be determined by dividing the aggregate area of rough openings for glazing (windows and glazed doors) in all the above grade walls associated with the building envelope by the total gross area of all above grade exterior walls that are a part for the building envelope. In buildings with multiple types of building envelope construction, each building envelope construction type shall be evaluated separately. Where Tables 802.2(1) through 802.2(7) do not list a particular construction type, the applicable provisions of ASHRAE/IESNA 90.1 shall be used in lieu of Section 802.

802.2.1 Above-grade walls. The minimum thermal resistance (*R*-value) of the insulating material(s) installed in the wall cavity between the framing members and continuously on the walls shall be as specified in Tables 802.2(1) through 802.2(7) based on framing type and construction materials used in the wall assembly. Where both cavity and continuous insulation values are provided in Tables 802.2(1) through 802.2(7), both requirements shall be met. Concrete masonry units (CMU) at least 8-inch (203 mm) nominal thickness with essentially equal amounts of mass on either side of the insulation layer are considered as having integral insulation; however, the thermal resistance of that insulation shall not be considered when determining compliance with Tables 802.2(1) through 802.2(7). "Other masonry walls" shall include walls weighing at least 35 lb/ft² (170kg/m²) of wall surface area and do not include CMUs less than 8 inches (203 mm) nominal thickness.

802.2.2 Nonglazed doors. Nonglazed doors shall meet the applicable requirements for windows and glazed doors and be considered part of the gross area of above-grade walls that are part of the building envelope.

802.2.3 Windows and glass doors. The maximum solar heat gain coefficient (SHGC) and thermal transmittance (U-factor) of window assemblies and glass doors located in the building envelope shall be as specified in Tables 802.2(1) through 802.2(7) based on the window projection factor.

The window projection factor shall be determined in accordance with Equation 8-1.

$$PF = A/B \qquad \textbf{(Equation 8-1)}$$

where:

PF = Projection factor (decimal).

A = Distance measured horizontally from the furthest continuous extremity of any overhang, eave or permanently attached shading device to the vertical surface of the glazing.

B = Distance measured vertically from the bottom of the glazing of the underside of the overhang, eave or permanently attached shading device.

Where different windows or glass doors have different PF values, they shall each be evaluated separately, or an area-weighted PF value shall be calculated and used for all windows and glass doors.

802.2.4 Roof assembly. The minimum thermal resistance (R-value) of the insulating material installed either between the roof framing or continuously on the roof assembly shall be as specified in Tables 802.2(1) through 802.2(7) based on construction materials used in the roof assembly.

802.2.5 Skylights. Skylights located in the building envelope shall be limited to 3 percent of the gross roof assembly area and shall have a maximum thermal transmittance (U-factor) of the skylight assembly as specified in Tables 802.2(1) through 802.2(7).

802.2.6 Floors over outdoor air or unconditioned space. The minimum thermal resistance (R-value) of the insulating material installed either between the floor framing or continuously on the floor assembly shall be as specified in Tables 802.2(1) through 802.2(7) based on construction materials used in the floor assembly.

802.2.7 Slabs on grade. The minimum thermal resistance (R-value) of the insulation around the perimeter of the slab floor shall be as specified in Tables 802.2(1) through 802.2(7). The insulation shall be placed on the outside of the foundation or on the inside of a foundation wall. The insulation shall extend downward from the top of the slab for a minimum of 48 inches (1219 mm) or downward to at least the bottom of the slab and then horizontally to the interior or exterior for a minimum total distance of 48 inches (1219 mm).

802.2.8 Below-grade walls. The minimum thermal resistance (R-value) of the insulating material installed in, or continuously on, the below-grade walls shall be as specified in Tables 802.2(1) through 802.2(7) and shall extend to a depth of 10 feet (3048 mm) below the outside finish ground level, or to the level of the floor, whichever is less.

802.2.9 Interior walls. The minimum thermal resistance (R-value) of the insulating material installed in the wall cavity or continuously on the interior walls shall be as specified in Table 802.2(1) for above-grade walls, regardless of glazing area, based on framing type and construction materials used in the wall assembly.

802.3 Air leakage. The requirements for air leakage shall be as specified in Sections 802.3.1 and 802.3.6.

802.3.1 Window, door and curtain wall assemblies. Window, sliding or swinging doors and curtain wall assemblies that are part of the building envelope shall be tested and listed as meeting AAMA/WDMA 101/I.S.2.

Exception: Site-constructed windows and doors that are weatherstripped or sealed in accordance with Section 802.3.2.

Commercial entrance doors shall have a maximum air infiltration rate of 1.75 cubic feet per minute (cfm)/ft^2 (32.0 m^3/h · m^2) of door area when tested in accordance with ASTM E 283.

802.3.2 Sealing of the building envelope. Openings and penetrations in the building envelope shall be sealed with caulking materials or closed with gasketing systems compatible with the construction materials and location. Joints and seams shall be sealed in the same manner or taped or covered with a moisture vapor-permeable wrapping material. Sealing materials spanning joints between construction materials shall allow for expansion and contraction of the construction materials.

802.3.3 Dampers integral to the building envelope. Stair, elevator shaft vents and other dampers integral to the building envelope shall be equipped with motorized dampers with a maximum leakage rate of 3 cfm/ft^2 at 1.0 in w.g. (250 Pa) when tested in accordance with AMCA 500. Such dampers shall be closed during normal building operation and shall open as required by fire and smoke detection systems.

Exception: Gravity (non-motorized) dampers are permitted to be used in buildings less than three stories in height above grade.

802.3.4 Loading dock weatherseals. Cargo doors and loading dock doors shall be equipped with weatherseals to restrict infiltration when vehicles are parked in the doorway.

802.3.5 Vestibules. A door that separates conditioned space from the exterior shall be protected with an enclosed vestibule, with all doors opening into and out of the vestibule equipped with self-closing devices. Vestibules shall be designed so that in passing through the vestibule it is not necessary for the interior and exterior doors to open at the same time.

Exceptions:

1. Doors not intended to be used as a building entrance door, such as doors to mechanical or electrical equipment rooms.

2. Doors opening directly from a guest room or dwelling unit.

3. Doors that open directly from a space less than 3,000 ft^2 (298 m^2) in area.

4. Revolving doors.

5. Doors used primarily to facilitate vehicular movement or material handling and adjacent personnel doors.

802.3.6 Recessed lighting fixtures. When installed in the building envelope, recessed lighting fixtures shall meet one of the following requirements:

1. Type IC rated, manufactured with no penetrations between the inside of the recessed fixture and ceiling cavity and sealed or gasketed to prevent air leakage into the unconditioned space.

2. Type IC or non-IC rated, installed inside a sealed box constructed from a minimum 0.5-inch-thick (12.7 mm) gypsum wallboard or constructed from a preformed polymeric vapor barrier, or other air-tight assembly manufactured for this purpose, while maintaining required clearances of not less than 0.5 inch (12.7 mm) from combustible material and not less than 3 inches (76 mm) from insulation material.

3. Type IC rated, in accordance with ASTM E 283 admitting no more than 2.0 cfm (0.944 L/s) of air movement from the conditioned space to the ceiling cavity. The lighting fixture shall be tested at 1.57 lbs/ft^2 (75 Pa) pressure difference and shall be labeled.

SECTION 803
BUILDING MECHANICAL SYSTEMS

803.1 General. This section covers the design and construction of mechanical systems and equipment serving the building heating, cooling or venting needs.

803.1.1 Compliance. Compliance with Section 803 shall be achieved by meeting either Section 803.2 or 803.3.

803.2 Simple HVAC systems and equipment. This section applies to buildings served by unitary or packaged HVAC equipment listed in Tables 803.2.2(1) through 803.2.2(5), each serving one zone and controlled by a single thermostat in the zone served. It also applies to two-pipe heating systems serving one or more zones, where no cooling system is installed.

This section does not apply to fan systems serving multiple zones, nonunitary or nonpackaged HVAC equipment and systems or hydronic or steam heating and hydronic cooling equipment and distribution systems that provide cooling or cooling and heating which are covered by Section 803.3.

803.2.1 Calculation of heating and cooling loads. Design loads shall be determined in accordance with the procedures described in Chapters 27 and 28 of the ASHRAE *Handbook of Fundamentals* or an approved equivalent computation procedure.

803.2.1.1 Equipment and system sizing. Heating and cooling equipment and systems capacity shall not exceed the loads calculated in accordance with Section 803.2.1. A single piece of equipment providing both heating and cooling must satisfy this provision for one function with the capacity for the other function as small as possible, within available equipment options.

803.2.2 HVAC equipment performance requirements. Equipment shall meet the minimum efficiency requirements of Tables 803.2.2(1), 803.2.2(2), 803.2.2(3), 803.2.2(4) and 803.2.2(5), when tested and rated in accordance with the applicable test procedure. The efficiency shall be verified through data furnished by the manufacturer or through certification under an approved certification program. Where multiple rating conditions or performance requirements are provided, the equipment shall satisfy all stated requirements.

803.2.3 Temperature and humidity controls. Requirements for temperature and humidity controls shall be as specified in Sections 803.2.3.1 and 803.2.3.2.

803.2.3.1 Temperature controls. Each heating and cooling system shall have at least one solid-state programmable thermostat. The thermostat shall have the capability to set back or shut down the system based on day of the week and time of day, and provide a readily accessible manual override that will return to the presetback or shutdown schedule without reprogramming. Heat pumps having supplementary electric resistance heat shall have controls that, except during defrost, prevent supplemental heat operation when the heat pump can meet the heating load.

803.2.3.2 Humidity controls. When humidistats are installed, they shall prevent the use of fossil fuel or electric power to achieve a humidity below 60 percent when the system controlled is cooling, and above 30 percent when the system controlled is heating.

TABLE 803.2.2(1)

ACCEPTABLE PRACTICE FOR COMMERCIAL BUILDINGS

TABLE 803.2.2(1)
UNITARY AIR CONDITIONERS AND CONDENSING UNITS, ELECTRICALLY OPERATED,
MINIMUM EFFICIENCY REQUIREMENTS

EQUIPMENT TYPE	SIZE CATEGORY	SUB-CATEGORY OR RATING CONDITION	MINIMUM EFFICIENCY[b]	TEST PROCEDURE[a]
Air conditioners, air cooled	< 65,000 Btu/h[d]	Split system	10.0 SEER	ARI 210/240
		Single package	9.7 SEER	
	≥ 65,000 Btu/h and < 135,000 Btu/h	Split system and single package	10.3 EER[c]	
	≥ 135,000 Btu/h and < 240,000 Btu/h	Split system and single package	9.7 EER[c]	ARI 340/360
	≥ 240,000 Btu/h and < 760,000 Btu/h	Split system and single package	9.5 EER[c] 9.7 IPLV[c]	
	> 760,000 Btu/h	Split system and single package	9.2 EER[c] 9.4 IPLV[c]	
Air conditioners, water and evaporatively cooled	< 65,000 Btu/h	Split System and single package	12.1 EER	ARI 210/240
	≥ 65,000 Btu/h and < 135,000 Btu/h	Split system and single package	11.5 EER[c]	
	≥ 135,000 Btu/h and 240,000 Btu/h	Split system and single package	11.0 EER[c]	ARI 340/360
	> 240,000 Btu/h	Split system and single package	11.0 EER[c] 10.3 IPLV[c]	

For SI: 1 Btu/hr = 0.2931 W

a. Chapter 9 contains a complete specification of the referenced test procedure, including the referenced year version of the test procedure.

b. IPLVs are only applicable to equipment with capacity modulation.

c. Deduct 0.2 from the required EERs and IPLVs for units with a heating section other than electric resistance heat.

d. Single-phase air-cooled air conditioners < 65,000 Btu/h are regulated by the National Appliance Energy Conservation Act of 1987 (NAECA). SEER values are those set by NAECA.

TABLE 803.2.2(2)
UNITARY AND APPLIED HEAT PUMPS, ELECTRICALLY OPERATED,
MINIMUM EFFICIENCY REQUIREMENTS

EQUIPMENT TYPE	SIZE CATEGORY	SUB-CATEGORY OR RATING CONDITION	MINIMUM EFFICIENCY[b]	TEST PROCEDURE[a]
Air cooled, (cooling mode)	< 65,000 Btu/h[d]	Split system	10.0 SEER	ARI 210/240
		Single package	9.7 SEER	
	≥ 65,000 Btu/h and < 135,000 Btu/h	Split system and single package	10.1 EER[c]	
	≥ 135,000 Btu/h and < 240,000 Btu/h	Split system and single package	9.3 EER[c]	ARI 340/360
	> 240,000 Btu/h	Split system and single package	9.0 EER[c] 9.2 IPLV[c]	
Water-source (cooling mode)	< 17,000 Btu/h	85°F entering water		ARI 320
		86°F entering water	11.2 EER	ISO-13256-1
	≥ 17,000 Btu/h and < 65,000 Btu/h	85°F entering water		ARI 320
		86°F entering water	12.0 EER	ISO-13256-1
	≥ 65,000 Btu/h and < 135,000 Btu/h	85°F entering water		ARI 320
		86°F entering water	12.0 EER	ISO-13256-1
Groundwater-source (cooling mode)	< 135,000 Btu/h	70°F entering water 50°F entering water		ARI 325
		59°F entering water	16.2 EER	ISO-13256-1
Ground source (cooling mode)	< 135,000 Btu/h	77°F entering brine 70°F entering brine		ARI 330
		77°F entering water	13.4 EER	ISO-13256-1
Air cooled (heating mode)	< 65,000 Btu/h[d] (Cooling capacity)	Split system	6.8 HSPF	ARI 210/240
		Single package	6.6 HSPF	
	≥ 65,000 Btu/h and < 135,000 Btu/h (Cooling capacity)	47°F db/43°F wb outdoor air	3.2 COP	
	>135,000 Btu/h (Cooling capacity)	47°F db/43°F wb outdoor air	3.1 COP	ARI 340/360
Water-source (heating mode)	< 135,000 Btu/h (Cooling capacity)	70°F entering water		ARI 320
		68°F entering water	4.2 COP	ISO-13256-1
Groundwater-source (heating mode)	< 135,000 Btu/h (Cooling capacity)	70°F entering water 50°F entering water		ARI 325
		50°F entering water	3.6 COP	ISO-13256-1
Ground source (heating mode)	< 135,000 Btu/h (Cooling capacity)	32°F entering brine		ARI 330
		32°F entering water	3.1 COP	ISO-13256-1

For SI: °C = [(°F) - 32] / 1.8, 1 Btu/h = 0.2931W

a. Chapter 9 contains a complete specification of the referenced test procedure, including the referenced year version of the test procedure.

b. IPLVs and Part load rating conditions are only applicable to equipment with capacity modulation.

c. Deduct 0.2 from the required EERs and IPLVs for units with a heating section other than electric resistance heat.

d. Single-phase air-cooled heat pumps < 65,000 Btu/h are regulated by the National Appliance Energy Conservation Act of 1987 (NAECA). SEER and HSPF values are those set by NAECA.

TABLE 803.2.2(3)
PACKAGED TERMINAL AIR CONDITIONERS AND PACKAGED TERMINAL HEAT PUMPS

EQUIPMENT TYPE	SIZE CATEGORY (INPUT)	SUB-CATEGORY OR RATING CONDITION	MINIMUM EFFICIENCY[b]	TEST PROCEDURE[a]
PTAC (cooling mode) new construction	All capacities	95°F db outdoor air	12.5 - (0.213 x Cap/1000) EER	ARI 310/380
PTAC (cooling mode) replacements[c]	All capacities	95°F db outdoor air	10.9 - (0.213 x Cap/1000) EER	
PTHP (cooling mode) new construction	All capacities	95°F db outdoor air	12.3 - (0.213 x Cap/1000) EER	
PTHP (cooling mode) replacements[c]	All capacities	95°F db outdoor air	10.8 - (0.213 x Cap/1000) EER	
PTHP (heating mode) new construction	All capacities		3.2 - (0.026 x Cap/1000) COP	
PTHP (heating mode) replacements[c]	All capacities		2.9 - (0.026 x Cap/1000) COP	

For SI: °C = [(°F) - 32] / 1.8, 1 Btu/h = 0.2931W

a. Chapter 9 contains a complete specification of the referenced test procedure, including the referenced year version of the test procedure.

b. Cap means the rated cooling capacity of the product in Btu/h. If the unit's capacity is less than 7,000 Btu/h, use 7,000 Btu/h in the calculation. If the unit's capacity is greater than 15,000 Btu/h, use 15,000 Btu/h in the calculation.

c. Replacement units must be factory labeled as follows: "MANUFACTURED FOR REPLACEMENT APPLICATIONS ONLY; NOT TO BE INSTALLED IN NEW CONSTRUCTION PROJECTS." Replacement efficiencies apply only to units with existing sleeves less than 16-in. (406 mm) high and less than 42-in. (1067 mm) wide.

TABLE 803.2.2(4)
WARM AIR FURNACES AND COMBINATION WARM AIR FURNACES/AIR-CONDITIONING UNITS, WARM AIR DUCT FURNACES AND UNIT HEATERS, MINIMUM EFFICIENCY REQUIREMENTS

EQUIPMENT TYPE	SIZE CATEGORY (INPUT)	SUB-CATEGORY OR RATING CONDITION	MINIMUM EFFICIENCY[d,e]	TEST PROCEDURE[a]
Warm air furnace, gas-fired	< 225,000 Btu/h		78% AFUE or 80% E_t[c]	DOE 10 CFR Part 430 or ANSI Z21.47
	≥ 225,000 Btu/h	Maximum capacity[c]	80% E_c[f]	ANSI Z21.47
Warm air furnace, oil-fired	< 225,000 Btu/h		78% AFUE or 80% E_t[c]	DOE 10 CFR Part 430 or UL 727
	≥ 225,000 Btu/h	Maximum capacity[b]	81% E_t[g]	UL 727
Warm air duct furnaces, gas-fired	All capacities	Maximum capacity[b] / Minimum capacity[b]	80% E_c / ———	ANSI Z83.9
Warm air unit heaters, gas-fired	All capacities	Maximum capacity[b] / Minimum capacity[b]	80% E_c / ———	ANSI Z83.8
Warm air unit heaters, oil-fired	All capacities	Maximum capacity[b] / Minimum capacity[b]	80% E_c / ———	UL 731

For SI: 1 Btu/h = 0.2931W

a. Chapter 9 contains a complete specification of the referenced test procedure, including the referenced year version of the test procedure.

b. Minimum and maximum ratings as provided for and allowed by the unit's controls.

c. Combination units not covered by the National Appliance Energy Conservation Act of 1987 (NAECA) (3-phase power or cooling capacity greater than or equal to 65,000 Btu/h [19 kW]) shall comply with either rating.

d. E_t = Thermal efficiency. See test procedure for detailed discussion.

e. E_c = Combustion efficiency (100% less flue losses). See test procedure for detailed discussion.

f. E_c = Combustion efficiency. Units must also include an IID, have jacket losses not exceeding 0.75% of the input rating and have either power venting or a flue damper. A vent damper is an acceptable alternative to a flue damper for those furnaces where combustion air is drawn from the conditioned space.

g. E_t = Thermal efficiency. Units must also include an IID, have jacket losses not exceeding 0.75% of the input rating and have either power venting or a flue damper. A vent damper is an acceptable alternative to a flue damper for those furnaces where combustion air is drawn from the conditioned space.

803.2.4 Hydronic system controls. Hydronic systems of at least 600,000 British thermal units per hour (Btu/h) (175 860 W) design capacity supplying heated water to comfort conditioning systems shall include controls that meet the requirements of Section 803.3.3.7.

803.2.5 Ventilation. Ventilation, either natural or mechanical, shall be provided in accordance with the *Mechanical Code of New York State*. Where mechanical ventilation is provided, the system shall provide the capability to reduce the outdoor air supply to the minimum required by the *Mechanical Code of New York State.*

803.2.6 Cooling with outdoor air. Each system over 65,000 Btu/h (19 kW) cooling capacity shall have an economizer that will automatically shut off the cooling system and allow all of the supply air to be provided directly from outdoors.

Economizers shall be capable of operating at 100 percent outside air, even if additional mechanical cooling is required to meet the cooling load of the building. Where a single room or space is supplied by multiple air systems, the aggregate capacity of those systems shall be used in applying this requirement.

Exceptions:

1. Where the cooling equipment is covered by the minimum efficiency requirements of Table 803.2.2(1) or 803.2.2(2) and meets the efficiency requirements of Table 803.2.6.
2. Systems with air or evaporatively cooled condensers and that serve spaces with open case refrigeration or that require filtration equipment in order to meet the minimum ventilation requirements of the *Mechanical Code of New York State.*
3. Systems under 135,000 Btu/h (40 kW) cooling capacity in Climate Zones 3c, 5b, 7, 13b and 14a and b.

803.2.7 Shutoff dampers. Outdoor air supply and exhaust ducts shall be provided with automatic means to reduce and shut off airflow.

Exceptions:

1. Systems serving areas designed for continuous operation.
2. Individual systems with a maximum 3,000 cfm (1416 L/s) airflow rate.
3. Systems with readily accessible manual dampers.
4. Where restricted by health and life safety codes.

803.2.8 Duct and plenum insulation and sealing. All supply and return air ducts and plenums shall be insulated with a minimum of R-5 insulation when located in unconditioned spaces and with a minimum of R-8 insulation when located outside the building envelope. When located within a building envelope assembly, the duct or plenum shall be separated from the building exterior or unconditioned or exempt spaces by a minimum of R-8 insulation.

Exceptions:

1. When located within equipment.
2. When the design temperature difference between the interior and exterior of the duct or plenum does not exceed 15°F (8°C).

All joints, longitudinal and transverse seams, and connections in ductwork, shall be securely fastened and sealed with welds, gaskets, mastics (adhesives), mastic-plus-embedded-fabric systems or tapes. Tapes and mastics used to seal ductwork shall be listed and labeled in accordance with UL 181A or UL 181B. Duct connections to flanges of air distribution system equipment shall be sealed and mechanically fastened. Unlisted duct tape is not permitted as a sealant on any metal ducts.

803.2.8.1 Duct construction. Duct work shall be constructed and erected in accordance with the *Mechanical Code of New York State.*

803.2.8.1.1 High- and medium-pressure duct systems. All ducts and plenums operating at a static pressure greater than 2 inches w.g. (500 Pa) shall be insulated and sealed in accordance with Section 803.2.8. Ducts operating at a static pressure in excess of 3 inches w.g. (750 Pa) shall be leak tested in accordance with Section 803.3.6. Pressure classifications specific to the duct system shall be clearly indicated on the construction documents in accordance with the *Mechanical Code of New York State.*

803.2.8.1.2 Low-pressure duct systems. All longitudinal and transverse joints, seams and connections of supply and return ducts operating at a static pressure less than or equal to 2 inches w.g. (500 Pa) shall be securely fastened and sealed with welds, gaskets, mastics (adhesives), mastic-plus-embedded fabric systems or tapes installed in accordance with the manufacturer's installation instructions. Pressure classifications specific to the duct system shall be clearly indicated on the construction documents in accordance with the *Mechanical Code of New York State.*

Exception: Continuously welded and locking-type longitudinal joints and seams on ducts operating at static pressures less than 2 inches w.g. (500 Pa) pressure classification.

803.2.9 Piping insulation. All piping serving as part of a heating or cooling system shall be thermally insulated in accordance with Section 803.3.7.

803.3 Complex HVAC systems and equipment. This section applies to buildings served by HVAC equipment and systems not covered in Section 803.2.

803.3.1 Calculation of heating and cooling loads. Design loads shall be determined in accordance with Section 803.2.1.

803.3.1.1 Equipment and system sizing. Heating and cooling equipment and system capacity shall not exceed the loads calculated in accordance with Section 803.2.1.

Exceptions:

1. Required standby equipment and systems provided with controls and devices that allow such systems or equipment to operate automatically only when the primary equipment is not operating.

TABLE 803.2.2(5) – 803.3.2   ACCEPTABLE PRACTICE FOR COMMERCIAL BUILDINGS

TABLE 803.2.2(5)
BOILERS, GAS- AND OIL-FIRED, MINIMUM EFFICIENCY REQUIREMENTS

EQUIPMENT TYPE[f]	SIZE CATEGORY (INPUT)	SUB-CATEGORY OR RATING CONDITION	MINIMUM EFFICIENCY[d]	TEST PROCEDURE
Boilers, gas-fired	< 300,000 Btu/h	Hot water	80% AFUE	DOE 10 CFR Part 430
		Steam	75% AFUE	
	≥ 300,000 Btu/h and ≤ 2,500,000 Btu/h	Maximum capacity[b]	75% E_t	H.I. HBS 86
	> 2,500,000 Btu/h[f]	Hot water	80% E_c	
		Steam	80% E_c	
Boilers, oil-fired	< 300,000 Btu/h		80% AFUE	DOE 10 CFR Part 430
	≥ 300,000 Btu/h and ≤ 2,500,000 Btu/h	Maximum capacity[b]	78% E_t	H.I. HBS 86
	> 2,500,000 Btu/h[f]	Hot water	83% E_c	
		Steam	83% E_c	
Oil-fired (Residual)	≥ 300,000 Btu/h and ≤ 2,500,000 Btu/h	Maximum capacity[b]	78% E_t	H.I. HBS 86
	> 2,500,000 Btu/h[f]	Hot water	83% E_c	
		Steam	83% E_c	

For SI: 1 Btu/h = 0.2931 W.

a. Chapter 9 contains a complete specification of the referenced test procedure, including the referenced year version of the test procedure.

b. Minimum and maximum ratings as provided for and allowed by the unit's controls.

c. E_c = Combustion efficiency (100% less flue losses). See reference document for detailed information.

d. E_t = Thermal efficiency. See reference document for detailed information.

e. Alternate test procedures used at the manufacturer's option are ASME PTC-4.1 for units over 5,000,000 Btu/h input, or ANSI Z21.13 for units greater than or equal to 300,000 Btu/h and less than or equal to 2,500,000 Btu/h input.

f. These requirements apply to boilers with rated input of 8,000,000 Btu/h or less that are not packaged boilers and to all packaged boilers. Minimum efficiency requirements for boilers cover all capacities of packaged boilers.

TABLE 803.2.6
MINIMUM EQUIPMENT EFFICIENCY ECONOMIZER EXCEPTION

TOTAL COOLING CAPACITY OF EQUIPMENT	BUILDING LOCATION		
	Zones 6a, 9a, 10a, 11a, 12a, 12b, 13a, 13b, 14a, 14b, 15-19	Zones 3a, 3b, 4a, 7a, 8, 9b, 10b, 11b	Zones 4b, 5a, 5b, 6b, 7b
90,000 Btu/h to 134,999 Btu/h	NA	11.4 EER	10.4 EER
135,000 Btu/h to 759,999 Btu/h	NA	10.9 EER	9.9 EER
760,000 Btu/h or more	NA	10.5 EER	9.6 EER

For SI: °C = [(°F)-32]/1.8, 1 Btu/h = 0.2931 W.

NA = Not Applicable.

2. Multiple units of the same equipment type with combined capacities exceeding the design load and provided with controls that have the capability to sequence the operation of each unit based on load.

803.3.2 HVAC equipment performance requirements. Equipment shall meet the minimum efficiency requirements of Tables 803.3.2(1) through 803.3.2(6) and Table 803.2.2(5), when tested and rated in accordance with the applicable test procedure. The efficiency shall be verified through certification under an approved certification program or, if no certification program exists, the equipment efficiency ratings shall be supported by data furnished by the manufacturer. Where multiple rating conditions or performance requirements are provided, the equipment shall satisfy all stated requirements. Where components, such as indoor or outdoor coils, from different manufacturers are used, calculations and supporting data shall be furnished by the designer that demonstrate the combined efficiency of the specified components meets the requirements herein.

Where unitary or prepackaged equipment is used in a complex HVAC system and is not covered by Section 803.3.2, the equipment shall meet the applicable requirements of Section 803.2.2.

Exception: Equipment listed in Table 803.3.2(2) not designed for operation at ARI Standard test conditions of 44°F (7°C) leaving chilled water temperature and 85°F (29°C) entering condenser water temperature shall have a minimum full load COP and IPLV rating as shown in Tables 803.3.2(3) through 803.3.2(5) as applicable. The table values are only applicable over the following full load design ranges:

Leaving Chilled Water Temperature:	40 to 48°F (4°C to 9°C)
Entering Condenser Water Temperature:	75 to 85°F (24°C to 29°C)
Condensing Water Temperature Rise:	5 to 15°F (-15°C to -9°C)

Chillers designed to operate outside of these ranges are not covered by this code.

803.3.3 HVAC system controls. Each heating and cooling system shall be provided with thermostatic controls as required in Sections 803.3.3.1 through 803.3.3.5.

803.3.3.1 Thermostatic controls. The supply of heating and cooling energy to each zone shall be controlled by individual thermostatic controls capable of responding to temperature within the zone. Where humidification or dehumidification or both is provided, at least one humidity control device shall be provided for each humidity control system.

Exception: Independent perimeter systems that are designed to offset only building envelope heat losses or gains or both serving one or more perimeter zones also served by an interior system provided:

1. The perimeter system includes at least one thermostatic control zone for each building exposure having exterior walls facing only one orientation (within +/- 45°) for more than 50 contiguous feet (15.2 m) and,

2. The perimeter system heating and cooling supply is controlled by a thermostat(s) located within the zone(s) served by the system.

803.3.3.1.1 Heat pump supplementary heat. Heat pumps having supplementary electric resistance heat shall have controls that, except during defrost, prevent supplementary heat operation when the heat pump can meet the heating load.

803.3.3.2 Set point overlap restriction. Where used to control both heating and cooling, zone thermostatic controls shall provide a temperature range or deadband of at least 5°F (Δ 2.8 °C) within which the supply of heating and cooling energy to the zone is capable of being shut off or reduced to a minimum.

Exception: Thermostats requiring manual changeover between heating and cooling modes.

TABLE 803.3.2(1)
CONDENSING UNITS, ELECTRICALLY OPERATED,
MINIMUM EFFICIENCY REQUIREMENTS

EQUIPMENT TYPE	SIZE CATEGORY	MINIMUM EFFICIENCY[b]	TEST PROCEDURE[a]
Condensing units, air cooled	135,000 Btu/h	10.1 EER 11.2 IPLV	ARI 365
Condensing units, water or evaporatively cooled	135,000 Btu/h	13.1 EER 13.1 IPLV	ARI 365

For SI: 1 Btu/h = 0.2931W

a. Chapter 9 contains a complete specification of the referenced test procedure, including the referenced year version of the test procedure.

b. IPLVs are only applicable to equipment with capacity modulation.

TABLE 803.3.2(2)

ACCEPTABLE PRACTICE FOR COMMERCIAL BUILDINGS

TABLE 803.3.2(2)
WATER CHILLING PACKAGES, MINIMUM EFFICIENCY REQUIREMENTS

EQUIPMENT TYPE	SIZE CATEGORY	MINIMUM EFFICIENCY[b]	TEST PROCEDURE[a]
Air cooled, with condenser, electrically operated	< 150 tons	2.80 COP 2.80 IPLV	ARI 550 or ARI 590 as appropriate
	≥ 150 tons		
Air cooled, without condenser, electrically operated	All capacities	3.10 COP 3.10 IPLV	ARI 590
Water cooled, electrically operated, positive displacement (reciprocating)	All capacities	4.20 COP 4.65 IPLV	
Water cooled, electrically operated, positive displacement (rotary screw and scroll)	< 150 tons	4.45 COP 4.50 IPLV	ARI 550 or ARI 590 as appropriate
	≥ 150 tons and < 300 tons	4.90 COP 4.95 IPLV	
	≥ 300 tons	5.50 COP 5.60 IPLV	
Water cooled, electrically operated, centrifugal [c]	< 150 tons	5.00 COP 5.00 IPLV	ARI 550
	≥ 150 tons and < 300 tons	5.55 COP 5.55 IPLV	
	≥ 300 tons	6.10 COP 6.10 IPLV	
Air cooled absorption single effect	All capacities	0.60 COP	
Water cooled absorption single effect	All capacities	0.70 COP	
Absorption double effect, indirect-fired	All capacities	1.00 COP 1.05 IPLV	ARI 560
Absorption double effect, direct-fired	All capacities	1.00 COP 1.00 IPLV	

For SI: 1 Ton = 3.517 kW

a. Chapter 9 contains a complete specification of the referenced test procedure, including the referenced year version of the test procedure.

b. The chiller equipment requirements do not apply for chillers used in low temperature applications where the design leaving fluid temperature is less than or equal to 40°F (4°C).

TABLE 803.3.2(3)
COPS AND IPLVS FOR NON-STANDARD CENTRIFUGAL CHILLERS < 150 TONS

CENTRIFUGAL CHILLERS < 150 TONS COP$_{std}$ = 5.4								
			CONDENSER FLOW RATE					
			2 gpm/ton	2.5 gpm/ton	3 gpm/ton	4 gpm/ton	5 gpm/ton	6 gpm/ton
Leaving chilled water temperature (°F)	Entering condenser water temperature (°F)	Lift[a] (°F)	Required COP and IPLV					
46	75	29	6.00	6.27	6.48	6.80	7.03	7.20
45	75	30	5.92	6.17	6.37	6.66	6.87	7.02
44	75	31	5.84	6.08	6.26	6.53	6.71	6.86
43	75	32	5.75	5.99	6.16	6.40	6.58	6.71
42	75	33	5.67	5.90	6.06	6.29	6.45	6.57
41	75	34	5.59	5.82	5.98	6.19	6.34	6.44
46	80	34	5.59	5.82	5.98	6.19	6.34	6.44
40	75	35	5.50	5.74	5.89	6.10	6.23	6.33
45	80	35	5.50	5.74	5.89	6.10	6.23	6.33
44	80	36	5.41	5.66	5.81	6.01	6.13	6.22
43	80	37	5.31	5.57	5.73	5.92	6.04	6.13
42	80	38	5.21	5.48	5.64	5.84	5.95	6.04
41	80	39	5.09	5.39	5.56	5.76	5.87	5.95
46	85	39	5.09	5.39	5.56	5.76	5.87	5.95
40	80	40	4.96	5.29	5.47	5.67	5.79	5.86
45	85	40	4.96	5.29	5.47	5.67	5.79	5.86
44	85	41	4.83	5.18	5.40	5.59	5.71	5.78
43	85	42	4.68	5.07	5.28	5.50	5.62	5.70
42	85	43	4.51	4.94	5.17	5.41	5.54	5.62
41	85	44	4.33	4.80	5.05	5.31	5.45	5.53
40	85	45	4.13	4.65	4.92	5.21	5.35	5.44
Condenser DT[b]			14.04	11.23	9.36	7.02	5.62	4.68

For SI: °C = [(°F) - 32] / 1.8

a. Lift = Entering condenser water temperature °F – Leaving chilled water temperature °F

b. Condenser DT = Leaving condenser water temperature °F – Entering condenser water temperature °F

K_{adj} = 6.1507 - 0.30244(X) + 0.0062692(X)^2 - 0.000045595(X)

where X = Condenser DT + Lift

COP_{adj} = K_{adj} * COP_{std}

TABLE 803.3.2(4)

ACCEPTABLE PRACTICE FOR COMMERCIAL BUILDINGS

TABLE 803.3.2(4)
COPS AND IPLVS FOR NON-STANDARD CENTRIFUGAL CHILLERS > 150 TONS, ≤ 300 TONS

CENTRIFUGAL CHILLERS > 150 Tons, ≤ 300 Tons $COP_{std} = 5.55$								
			CONDENSER FLOW RATE					
			2 gpm/ton	2.5 gpm/ton	3 gpm/ton	4 gpm/ton	5 gpm/ton	6 gpm/ton
Leaving chilled water temperature (°F)	Entering condenser water temperature (°F)	Lift[a] (°F)	Required COP and IPLV					
46	75	29	6.17	6.44	6.66	6.99	7.23	7.40
45	75	30	6.08	6.34	6.54	6.84	7.06	7.22
44	75	31	6.00	6.24	6.43	6.71	6.90	7.05
43	75	32	5.91	6.15	6.33	6.58	6.76	6.89
42	75	33	5.83	6.07	6.23	6.47	6.63	6.75
41	75	34	5.74	5.98	6.14	6.36	6.51	6.62
46	80	34	5.74	5.98	6.14	6.36	6.51	6.62
40	75	35	5.65	5.90	6.05	6.26	6.40	6.51
45	80	35	5.65	5.90	6.05	6.26	6.40	6.51
44	80	36	5.56	5.81	5.97	6.17	6.30	6.40
43	80	37	5.46	5.73	5.89	6.08	6.21	6.30
42	80	38	5.35	5.64	5.80	6.00	6.12	6.20
41	80	39	5.23	5.54	5.71	5.91	6.03	6.11
46	85	39	5.23	5.54	5.71	5.91	6.03	6.11
40	80	40	5.10	5.44	5.62	5.83	5.95	6.03
45	85	40	5.10	5.44	5.62	5.83	5.95	6.03
44	85	41	4.96	5.33	5.55	5.74	5.86	5.94
43	85	42	4.81	5.21	5.42	5.66	5.78	5.86
42	85	43	4.63	5.08	5.31	5.56	5.69	5.77
41	85	44	4.45	4.93	5.19	5.46	5.60	5.69
40	85	45	4.24	4.77	5.06	5.35	5.50	5.59
Condenser DT[b]			14.04	11.23	9.36	7.02	5.62	4.68

For SI: °C = [(°F) - 32] / 1.8

a. Lift = Entering condenser water temperature °F – Leaving chilled water temperature °F

b. Condenser DT = Leaving condenser water temperature °F – Entering condenser water temperature °F

$K_{adj} = 6.1507 - 0.30244(X) + 0.0062692(X)^2 - 0.000045595(X)^3$

where X = Condenser DT + Lift

$COP_{adj} = K_{adj} * COP_{std}$

TABLE 803.3.2(5)
COPS AND IPLVS FOR NON-STANDARD CENTRIFUGAL CHILLERS > 300 TONS

			Condenser Flow Rate					
CENTRIFUGAL CHILLERS > 300 TONS **COP_std = 6.1**			2 gpm/ton	2.5 gpm/ton	3 gpm/ton	4 gpm/ton	5 gpm/ton	6 gpm/ton
Leaving chilled water temperature (°F)	**Entering condenser water temperature (°F)**	**Lift[a] (°F)**	Required COP and IPLV					
46	75	29	6.80	7.11	7.35	7.71	7.97	8.16
45	75	30	6.71	6.99	7.21	7.55	7.78	7.96
44	75	31	6.61	6.89	7.09	7.40	7.61	7.77
43	75	32	6.52	6.79	6.98	7.26	7.45	7.60
42	75	33	6.43	6.69	6.87	7.13	7.31	7.44
41	75	34	6.33	6.60	6.77	7.02	7.18	7.30
46	80	34	6.33	6.60	6.77	7.02	7.18	7.30
40	75	35	6.23	6.50	6.68	6.91	7.06	7.17
45	80	35	6.23	6.50	6.68	6.91	7.06	7.17
44	80	36	6.13	6.41	6.58	6.81	6.95	7.05
43	80	37	6.02	6.31	6.49	6.71	6.85	6.94
42	80	38	5.90	6.21	6.40	6.61	6.75	6.84
41	80	39	5.77	6.11	6.30	6.52	6.65	6.74
46	85	39	5.77	6.11	6.30	6.52	6.65	6.74
40	80	40	5.63	6.00	6.20	6.43	6.56	6.65
45	85	40	5.63	6.00	6.20	6.43	6.56	6.65
44	85	41	5.47	5.87	6.10	6.33	6.47	6.55
43	85	42	5.30	5.74	5.98	6.24	6.37	6.46
42	85	43	5.11	5.60	5.86	6.13	6.28	6.37
41	85	44	4.90	5.44	5.72	6.02	6.17	6.27
40	85	45	4.68	5.26	5.58	5.90	6.07	6.17
Condenser DT[b]			14.04	11.23	9.36	7.02	5.62	4.68

For SI: °C = [(°F) - 32] / 1.8

a. Lift = Entering condenser water temperature °F – Leaving chilled water temperature °F

b. Condenser DT = Leaving condenser water temperature °F – Entering condenser water temperature °F

$K_{adj} = 6.1507 - 0.30244(X) + 0.0062692(X)^2 - 0.000045595(X)^3$

where X = Condenser DT + Lift

$COP_{adj} = K_{adj} * COP_{std}$

TABLE 803.3.2(6) - 803.3.3.6

ACCEPTABLE PRACTICE FOR COMMERCIAL BUILDINGS

TABLE 803.3.2(6)
PERFORMANCE REQUIREMENTS FOR HEAT REJECTION EQUIPMENT

Equipment Type	Total System Heat Rejection Capacity at Rated Conditions	Sub-Category or Rating Condition	Performance	Test Procedure[c]
Propeller or axial fan cooling towers	All	95°F (35°C) entering water 85°F (29°C) leaving water 75°F (24°C) wb outdoor air	≥ 38.2 gpm/hp (3.23 L/s·kW)	CTI ATC-105 and CTI STD-201
Centrifugal fan cooling towers	All	95°F (35°C) entering water 85°F (29°C) leaving water 75°F (24°C) wb outdoor air	≥ 20.0 gpm/hp (1.7 L/s·kW)	CTI ATC-105 and CTI STD-201
Air cooled condensers	All	125°F (52°C) condensing temperature R22 Test Fluid 190°F (88°C) entering gas temperature 15°F (8°C) Subcooling 95°F (35°C) Entering drybulb	≥ 176,000 Btu/h·hp (69 COP)	ARI 460

For SI: °C = [(°F) - 32] / 1.8, 1 Btu/h = 0.2931W, 1 L/s·kW = 11.8 gpm/hp

a. For purposes of this table, cooling tower performance is defined as the maximum flow rating of the tower units (gpm) divided by the fan nameplate rated motor power units (hp).

b. For purposes of this table, air-cooled condenser performance is defined as the heat rejected from the refrigerant units (Btu/h) divided by the fan nameplate rated motor power units (hp).

c. Chapter 9 contains a complete specification of the referenced test procedure, including the referenced year version of the test procedure.

803.3.3.3 Off-hour controls. Each zone shall be provided with thermostatic setback controls that are controlled by either an automatic time clock or programmable control system.

Exceptions:

1. Zones that will be operated continuously.

2. Zones with a full HVAC load demand not exceeding 6,800 Btu/h (2 kW) and having a readily accessible manual shutoff switch.

803.3.3.3.1 Thermostatic setback capabilities. Thermostatic setback controls shall have the capability to set back or temporarily operate the system to maintain zone temperatures down to 55°F (13°C) or up to 85°F (29°C).

803.3.3.3.2 Automatic setback and shutdown capabilities. Automatic time clock or programmable controls shall be capable of starting and stopping the system for seven different daily schedules per week and retaining their programming and time setting during a loss of power for at least 10 hours. Additionally, the controls shall have: a manual override that allows temporary operation of the system for up to 2 hours; a manually operated timer capable of being adjusted to operate the system for up to 2 hours; or an occupancy sensor.

803.3.3.4 Shutoff damper controls. Both outdoor air supply and exhaust ducts shall be equipped with gravity or motorized dampers that will automatically shut when the systems or spaces served are not in use.

Exception: Individual supply systems with a design airflow rate of 3,000 cfm (1416 L/s) or less.

803.3.3.5 Economizers. Economizers shall be provided on each system over 65,000 Btu/h (19 kW) cooling capacity in accordance with Section 803.2.6.

Exceptions:

1. Water economizers that are capable of cooling supply air by direct and/or indirect evaporation and providing up to 100% of the expected system cooling load at outside air temperatures of 50°F (10°C) dry bulb/45°F (7.2°C) wet bulb and below.

2. Systems under 135,000 Btu/h (40 kW) cooling capacity in Climate Zones 3c, 5b, 7, 13b and 14a and b.

803.3.3.6 Variable air volume (VAV) fan control. Individual VAV fans with motors of 25 horsepower (hp) (18.8 kW) or greater shall be driven by a mechanical or electrical variable speed drive; be a vane-axial fan with variable pitch blades; or have controls or devices that will result in fan motor demand of no more than 50 percent of their design wattage at 50 percent of design airflow when static pressure set point equals one-third of the total design static pressure.

803.3.3.7 Hydronic systems controls. The heating of fluids that have previously been mechanically cooled and the cooling of fluids that have previously been mechanically heated shall be limited in accordance with Sections 803.3.3.7.1 through 803.3.3.7.3. Hydronic heating systems comprising multiple packaged boilers and designed to deliver conditioned water or steam into a common distribution system shall include automatic controls capable of sequencing operation of the boilers. Hydronic heating systems comprising a single boiler and greater than 500,000 Btu/h input design capacity shall include either a multi-staged or modulating burner.

803.3.3.7.1 Three-pipe system. Hydronic systems that use a common return system for both hot water and chilled water are prohibited.

803.3.3.7.2 Two-pipe changeover system. Systems that use a common distribution system to supply both heated and chilled water shall: be designed to allow a dead band between changeover from one mode to the other of at least 15°F (–9°C) outside air temperatures; be designed and be provided with controls to allow operation in one mode for at least 4 hours before changing over to the other mode; and be provided with controls that allow heating and cooling supply temperatures at the changeover point to be no more than 30°F (–1°C) apart.

803.3.3.7.3 Hydronic (water loop) heat pump systems. Hydronic heat pumps connected to a common heat pump water loop with central devices for heat rejection and heat addition shall have controls that are capable of providing a heat pump water supply temperature dead band of at least 20°F (–7°C) between initiation of heat rejection and heat addition by the central devices. If a close-circuit cooling tower is used, either an automatic valve shall be installed to bypass all but a minimal flow of water around the tower, or low leakage positive closure dampers shall be provided. If an open-circuit tower is used directly in the heat pump loop, an automatic valve shall be installed to bypass all heat pump water flow around the tower. If an open-circuit cooling tower is used in conjunction with a separate heat exchanger to isolate the cooling tower from the heat pump loop, then heat loss shall be controlled by shutting down the circulation pump on the cooling tower loop. Each hydronic heat pump on the hydronic system having a total pump system power exceeding 10 hp shall be a two-position valve.

> **Exception:** Where a system loop temperature optimization controller is installed and can determine the most efficient operating temperature based on real time conditions of demand and capacity, dead bands of less than 20°F (–7°C) shall be permitted.

803.3.3.7.4 Part load controls. Hydronic systems greater than or equal to 600,000 Btu/h (175 860 W) in design capacity supplying heated or chilled water to comfort conditioning systems shall include controls that have the capability to:

1. Automatically reset the supply water temperatures using zone return water temperature, building return water temperature, or outside air temperature as an indicator of building heating or cooling demand. The temperature shall be capable of being reset by at least 25 percent of the design supply-to-return water temperature difference; or

2. Reduce system pump flow by at least 50 percent of design flow rate utilizing adjustable speed drive(s) on pump(s), utilize multiple staged pumps where at least one-half of the total pump horsepower is capable of being automatically turned off, utilize control valves designed to modulate or step down, and close, as a function of load, or other approved means.

803.3.3.8 Heat rejection equipment fan speed control. Each fan powered by a motor of 7.5 hp (5.6 kW) or larger shall have the capability to operate that fan at two-thirds of full speed or less, and shall have controls that automatically change the fan speed to control the leaving fluid temperature or condensing temperature/pressure of the heat rejection device.

> **Exception:** Factory-installed heat rejection devices within HVAC equipment tested and rated in accordance with Tables 803.3.2(1) through 803.3.2(3).

803.3.4 Requirements for complex mechanical systems serving multiple zones. Systems serving multiple zones shall be VAV systems which, during periods of occupancy, are designed and capable of being controlled to reduce primary air supply to each zone to a minimum before reheating, recooling or mixing takes place. Sections 803.3.4.1 through 803.3.4.4 shall apply to complex mechanical systems.

Exceptions:

1. Zones where special pressurization relationships or cross-contamination requirements are such that VAV systems are impractical.

2. Where at least 75 percent of the energy for reheating or for providing warm air in mixing systems is provided from a site-recovered or site-solar energy source.

3. Zones where special humidity levels are required to satisfy process needs.

4. Zones with a peak supply air quantity of 300 cfm (142 L/s) or less and where the flow rate is less than 10 percent of the total fan system supply airflow rate.

5. Zones where the volume of air to be reheated, recooled, or mixed is no greater than the volume of outside air required to meet the minimum ventilation requirements of the *Mechanical Code of New York State*.

6. Systems with zone thermostatic and humidistatic controls capable of operating in sequence the supply of heating and cooling energy to the zone and which are capable of preventing reheating, recooling, mixing or simultaneous supply of air

that has been previously mechanically cooled and air that has been previously mechanically heated.

⇒ **803.3.4.1** Reserved.

803.3.4.2 Single duct variable air volume (VAV) systems, terminal devices. Single duct VAV systems shall use terminal devices capable of reducing the supply of primary supply air before reheating or recooling takes place.

803.3.4.3 Dual duct and mixing VAV systems, terminal devices. Systems that have one warm air duct and one cool air duct shall use terminal devices which are capable of reducing the flow from one duct to a minimum before mixing of air from the the the other duct takes place.

803.3.4.4 Single fan dual duct and mixing VAV systems, economizers. Individual dual duct or mixing heating and cooling systems with a single fan and with total capacities greater than 90,000 Btu/h [(26 375 W) 7.5 tons] shall not be equipped with air economizers.

803.3.5 Ventilation. Ventilation shall be in accordance with Section 803.2.5.

803.3.6 Duct and plenum insulation and sealing. All ducts and plenums shall be insulated and sealed in accordance with Section 803.2.8.

Ducts designed to operate at static pressures in excess of 3 inch water gauge (wg) (746 Pa) shall be leak-tested in accordance with the SMACNA *HVAC Air Duct Leakage Test Manual* with the rate of air leakage *(CL)* less than or equal to 6.0 as determined in accordance with Equation 8-2.

$$CL = F \times P^{0.65} \qquad \textbf{(Equation 8-2)}$$

where:

F = The measured leakage rate in cfm per 100 square feet of duct surface.

P = The static pressure of the test.

Documentation shall be furnished by the designer demonstrating that representative sections totaling at least 25 percent of the duct area have been tested and that all tested sections meet the requirements of this section.

803.3.7 Piping insulation. All piping serving as part of a heating or cooling system shall be thermally insulated in accordance with Table 803.3.7.

Exceptions:

1. Factory-installed piping within HVAC equipment tested and rated in accordance with a test procedure referenced by this code.

2. Piping that conveys fluids that have a design operating temperature range between 55°F (13°C) and 105°F (41°C).

3. Piping that conveys fluids that have not been heated or cooled through the use of fossil fuels or electric power.

4. Runout piping not exceeding 4 feet (1219 mm) in length and 1 inch (25 mm) in diameter between the control valve and HVAC coil.

TABLE 803.3.7
MINIMUM PIPE INSULATION[a]
(thickness in inches)

FLUID	NOMINAL PIPE DIAMETER	
	≤ 1.5"	> 1.5"
Steam	1.5	3.0
Hot water	1.0	2.0
Chilled water, brine or refrigerant	1.0	1.5

For SI: 1 inch = 25.4 mm, Btu per inch/h · ft² · °F = W per 25 mm/K · m².

a. Based on insulation having a conductivity not exceeding 0.27 Btu per inch/h · ft² · °F.

803.3.8 HVAC system completion. Prior to the issuance of a certificate of occupancy, the following shall be completed by the design professional.

803.3.8.1 Air system balancing. Each supply air outlet and zone terminal device shall be equipped with means for air balancing in accordance with the requirements of the *Mechanical Code of New York State*. Discharge dampers are prohibited on constant volume fans and variable volume fans with motors 25 hp and larger.

803.3.8.2 Hydronic system balancing. Individual hydronic heating and cooling coils shall be equipped with means for balancing and pressure test connections.

803.3.8.3 Manuals. The construction documents shall require an operating and maintenance manual be provided to the building owner by the mechanical contractor. The manual shall include, at least, the following:

1. Equipment capacity (input and output) and required maintenance actions.

2. Equipment operation and maintenance manuals.

3. HVAC system control maintenance and calibration information, including wiring diagrams, schematics and control sequence descriptions. Desired or field-determined setpoints shall be permanently recorded on control drawings, at control devices, or, for digital control systems, in programming comments.

4. A complete written narrative of how each system is intended to operate.

SECTION 804
SERVICE WATER HEATING

804.1 General. This section covers the minimum efficiency of and controls for service water-heating equipment and insulation of service hot water piping.

804.2 Service water-heating equipment performance efficiency. Water-heating equipment and hot water storage tanks shall meet the requirements of Table 504.2. The efficiency shall be verified through data furnished by the manufacturer or through certification under an approved certification program.

804.3 Temperature controls. Service water-heating equipment shall be provided with controls to allow a set point of 110°F (43°C) for equipment serving dwelling units and 90°F (32°C) for equipment serving other occupancies. The outlet temperature of lavatories in public facility rest rooms shall be limited to 110°F (43°C).

804.4 Heat traps. Water-heating equipment not supplied with integral heat traps and serving noncirculating systems shall be provided with heat traps on the supply and discharge piping associated with the equipment.

804.5 Pipe insulation. Piping on return circulation hot water systems shall be insulated with 1 inch (25 mm) of insulation having a conductivity not exceeding 0.28 Btu per inch/h · ft^2 · °F (1.59 W per 25 mm/m^2 · K). The first 8 feet (2438 mm) of piping in noncirculating systems served by equipment without integral heat traps shall be insulated with 0.5 inch (12.7 mm) of material having a conductivity not exceeding 0.28 Btu per inch/h · ft^2 · °F (1.59 W per 25 mm/m^2 · K).

804.6 Hot water system controls. Automatic circulating hot water systems or heat trace shall have time switches that are capable of being set to turn off the system.

SECTION 805
LIGHTING AND POWER SYSTEMS

805.1 General. This section covers lighting system controls, the connection of ballasts, the maximum lighting power for interior applications, minimum acceptable lighting equipment for exterior applications and transformer efficiencies.

Exception: Lighting within dwelling units.

805.2 Lighting controls. Lighting systems shall be provided with controls as required in Sections 805.2.1, 805.2.2 and 805.2.3.

805.2.1 Interior lighting controls. Each area enclosed by walls or floor-to-ceiling partitions shall have at least one manual control for the lighting serving that area. The required controls shall be located within the area served by the controls or be a remote switch that identifies the lights served and indicates their status.

Exceptions:

1. Areas designated as security or emergency areas that must be continuously lighted.

2. Lighting in stairways or corridors that are elements of the means of egress.

805.2.1.1 Additional controls. Each area that is required to have a manual control shall have additional controls that meet the requirements of Section 805.2.1.1.1, 805.2.1.1.2 or 805.2.1.1.3.

Exceptions:

1. Areas that have only 1 luminaire.

2. Areas that are controlled by an occupant-sensing device.

3. Corridors, storerooms, restrooms or public lobbies.

805.2.1.1.1 Bi-level switching. Each area less than 250 ft^2 (23 m^2) that is required to have a manual control shall also allow the occupant to reduce the connected lighting load in a reasonably uniform illumination pattern by at least 50 percent.

Exceptions:

1. Areas that have only 1 luminaire.

2. Areas that are controlled by an occupant-sensing device.

3. Corridors, storerooms, restrooms or public lobbies.

4. Guest rooms.

805.2.1.1.2 Automatic lighting shutoff. Spaces greater than 250 ft^2 (23 m^2) in buildings larger than 5,000 ft^2 (465 m^2) shall be equipped with an automatic control device to shut off lighting in those spaces. This automatic control device shall function on either:

1. A scheduled basis, using time-of-day, with an independent program schedule that controls the interior lighting in areas that do not exceed 25,000 ft^2 (2323 m^2) and are not more than one floor, or

2. An unscheduled basis by occupant intervention.

805.2.1.1.3 Guest rooms. Guest rooms in hotels, motels, boarding houses or similar buildings shall have at least one master switch at the main entry door that controls all permanently wired lighting fixtures and switched receptacles, except those in the bathroom(s). Suites shall have a control meeting these requirements at the entry to each room or at the primary entry to the suite.

805.2.2 Exterior lighting controls. Automatic switching or photocell controls shall be provided for all exterior lighting not intended for 24-hour operation. Automatic time switches shall have a combination seven-day and seasonal daylight program schedule adjustment, and a minimum 4-hour power backup.

805.3 Tandem wiring. One- or three-lamp fluorescent fixtures that are pendant- or surface-mounted in continuous rows or recess mounted in an accessible ceiling and within 10 feet (3048 mm) of each other shall be tandem wired.

Exceptions:

1. Where electronic high-frequency ballasts are used.

2. Luminaires not on the same switch control or in the same area.

805.4 Interior lighting power requirements. A building complies with this section if its total connected lighting power calculated under Section 805.4.1 is no greater than the interior lighting power calculated under Section 805.4.2.

805.4.1 Total connected interior lighting power. The total connected interior lighting power (watts) shall be the sum of the watts of all interior lighting equipment as determined according to Sections 805.4.1.1 through 805.4.1.4.

Exceptions: The connected power associated with the following lighting equipment is not included in calculating total connected lighting power.

1. Specialized medical, dental and research lighting.

2. Professional sports arena playing field lighting.

3. Display lighting for exhibits in galleries, museums and monuments.

4. Guest room lighting in hotels, motels, boarding houses or similar buildings.

5. Emergency lighting automatically off during normal building operation.

805.4.1.1 Screw lamp holders. The wattage shall be the maximum labeled wattage of the luminaire.

805.4.1.2 Low-voltage lighting. The wattage shall be the specified wattage of the transformer supplying the system.

805.4.1.3 Other luminaires. The wattage of all other lighting equipment shall be the wattage of the lighting equipment verified through data furnished by the manufacturer or other approved sources.

805.4.1.4 Line-voltage lighting track and plug-in busway. The wattage shall be the greater of the wattage of the luminaires determined according to Sections 805.4.1.1 through 805.4.1.3 or 30 W/linear feet (98W/lin m).

805.4.2 Interior lighting power. The interior lighting power shall be calculated using Section 805.4.2.1 or 805.4.2.2. as applicable.

805.4.2.1 Entire building method. Under this approach, the interior lighting power (watts) is the value from Table 805.4.2 for the building type times the conditioned floor area of the entire building.

805.4.2.2 Tenant area or portion of building method. The total interior lighting power (watts) is the sum of all interior lighting powers for all areas in the building covered in this permit. The interior lighting power is the conditioned floor area for each area type listed in Table 805.4.2 times the value from Table 805.4.2 for that area. For the purposes of this method, an "area" shall be defined as all contiguous spaces which accommodate or are associated with a single area type as listed in Table 805.4.2. When this method is used to calculate the total interior lighting power for an entire building, each area type shall be treated as a separate area.

805.5 Exterior lighting. When the power for exterior lighting is supplied through the energy service to the building, all exterior lighting, other than low-voltage landscape lighting, shall have a source efficacy of at least 45 lumens per watt.

Exception: Where approved because of historical, safety, signage or emergency considerations.

805.6 Transformers. Single-phase and three-phase dry-type and liquid-filled distribution transformers shall be selected based on rating as described in Sections 805.6.1 and 805.6.2.

Exceptions:

1. Liquid-filled transformers below 10 kVA or dry-type transformers below 15 kVA.
2. Drive transformers, both AC and DC.
3. All rectifier transformers and transformers designed for high harmonics.
4. Autotransformers.
5. Non-distribution transformers, such as UPS (Uninterruptible Power Supply) transformers.
6. Special impedance, regulation and harmonic transformers.
7. Sealed and non-ventilated transformers.
8. Retrofit transformers, machine tool transformers or welding transformers.
9. Transformers with tap ranges greater than 15 percent or with frequency other than 60 Hz.
10. Grounding or testing transformers.
11. Where the loading on the subject transformers can be demonstrated to be such that a different transformer would consume less energy.

805.6.1 Liquid-immersed transformers. Liquid-immersed transformers shall comply with the minimum efficiencies in Table 805.6.1 as tested and rated in accordance with Section 313 of the Electric Utility Industry Restructuring Act of November 25, 1997 (NEMA TP 1).

805.6.2 Dry-type transformers. Dry-type transformers shall comply with the minimum efficiencies in Table 805.6.2 as tested and rated in accordance with NEMA TP 1.

SECTION 806
TOTAL BUILDING PERFORMANCE

806.1 General. The proposed design complies with this section where annual energy costs of the Proposed design as determined in accordance with Section 806.3 do not exceed those of the Standard design as determined in accordance with Section 806.4.

806.2 Analysis procedures. Sections 806.2.1 through 806.2.8 shall be applied in determining total building performance.

806.2.1 Energy analysis. Annual (8,760 hours) energy costs for the Standard design and the Proposed design shall each be determined using the same approved energy analysis simulation tool.

TABLE 805.4.2
INTERIOR LIGHTING POWER

BUILDING OR AREA TYPE	ENTIRE BUILDING (W/ft²)	TENANT AREA OR PORTION OF BUILDING (W/ft²)
Auditorium	NA	1.6
Bank/financial institution[a]	NA	2.0
Classroom/lecture hall[b]	NA	1.6
Convention, conference or meeting center[a]	NA	1.5
Corridor, restroom, support area	NA	0.8
Dining[a]	NA	1.4
Exercise center[a]	1.4	1.1
Exhibition hall	NA	3.3
Grocery store[c]	1.9	2.1
Gymnasium playing surface	NA	1.9
Hotel function[a]	NA	2.4
Industrial work, < 20 ft ceiling height	NA	2.1
Industrial work, ≥ 20 ft ceiling height	NA	3.0
Kitchen	NA	2.2
Library[a]	1.5	1.8
Lobby—hotel[a]	NA	1.9
Lobby—other[a]	NA	1.0
Mall, arcade or atrium	NA	1.4
Medical and clinical care[b, d]	1.6	1.6
Museum[b]	1.6	1.6
Office[b]	1.3	1.5
Religious worship[a]	2.2	3.2
Restaurant[a]	1.7	1.7
Retail sales, wholesale showroom[c]	1.9	2.1
School	1.5	NA
Storage, industrial and commercial	0.6	1.0
Theaters—motion picture	1.1	1.0
Theaters—performance[a]	1.4	1.5
Other	0.6	1.0

For SI: 1 foot = 304.8 mm, 1 W/ft² = W/0.0929 m².

NA = Not Applicable

a. Where lighting equipment is specified to be installed for decorative appearances in addition to lighting equipment specified for general lighting and is switched or dimmed on circuits different from the circuits for general lighting, the smaller of the actual wattage of the decorative lighting equipment or 1.0 W/ft² times the area of the space that the decorative lighting equipment is in shall be added to the interior lighting power determined in accordance with this line item.

b. Where lighting equipment is specified to be installed to meet requirements of visual display terminals as the primary viewing task, the smaller of the actual wattage of the lighting equipment or 0.35 W/ft² times the area of the space that the lighting equipment is in shall be added to the interior lighting power determined in accordance with this line item.

c. Where lighting equipment is specified to be installed to highlight specific merchandise in addition to lighting equipment specified for general lighting and is switched or dimmed on circuits different from the circuits for general lighting, the smaller of the actual wattage of the lighting equipment installed specifically for merchandise, or 1.6 W/ft² times the area of the specific display, or 3.9 W/ft² times the actual case or shelf area for displaying and selling fine merchandise such as jewelry, fine apparel and accessories, or china and silver, shall be added to the interior lighting power determined in accordance with this line item.

d. Where lighting equipment is specified to be installed, the smaller of the actual wattage of the lighting equipment, or 1.0 W/ft² times the area of the emergency, recovery, medical supply and pharmacy space shall be added to the interior lighting power determined in accordance with this line item.

TABLE 805.6.1 – 806.2.4

ACCEPTABLE PRACTICE FOR COMMERCIAL BUILDINGS

TABLE 805.6.1
NEMA CLASS 1 EFFICIENCY LEVELS FOR LIQUID-FILLED DISTRIBUTION TRANSFORMERS

REFERENCE CONDITION		TEMPERATURE		% OF NAMEPLATE LOAD
Load Loss No Load Loss		85°C 20°C		50% 50%
kVA	Single-Phase Efficiency		VA	Three-Phase Efficiency
10	98.3		15	98.0
15	98.5		30	98.3
25	98.7		45	98.5
37.5	98.8		75	98.7
50	98.9		112.5	98.8
75	99.0		150	98.9
100	99.0		225	99.0
167	99.1		300	99.0
250	99.2		500	99.1
333	99.2		750	99.2
500	99.3		1000	99.2
667	99.4		1500	99.3
883	99.4		2000	99.4
			2500	99.4

TABLE 805.6.2
NEMA CLASS 1 EFFICIENCY LEVELS FOR DRY-TYPE DISTRIBUTION TRANSFORMERS

REFERENCE CONDITION			TEMPERATURE		% OF NAMEPLATE LOAD
Low Voltage Medium Voltage			75°C 75°C		35% 50%
Single-Phase Efficiency			Three-Phase Efficiency		
kVa	Low Voltage	Medium Voltage	kVa	Low Voltage	Medium Voltage
15	97.7	97.6	15	97.0	96.8
25	98.0	97.7	30	97.5	97.3
37.5	98.2	98.1	45	97.7	97.6
50	98.3	98.2	75	98.0	97.9
75	98.5	98.4	112.5	98.2	98.1
100	98.6	98.5	150	98.3	98.2
167	98.7	98.7	225	98.5	98.4
250	98.8	98.8	300	98.6	98.5
333	98.9	98.9	500	98.7	98.7
500	—	99.0	750	98.8	98.8
667	—	99.0	1000	98.9	98.9
833	—	99.1	1500	—	99.0
			2000	—	99.0
			2500	—	99.1

806.2.2 Climate data. The climate data used in the energy analysis shall cover a full calendar year (8,760 hours) and shall reflect approved coincident hourly data for temperature, solar radiation, humidity and wind speed for the building location.

806.2.3 Energy rates. The annual energy costs shall be estimated using energy rates published by the serving energy supplier and which would apply to the actual building or *DOE State-Average Energy Prices* published by DOE's Energy Information Administration and which would apply to the actual building.

806.2.4 Nondepletable energy. Nondepletable energy collected offsite shall be treated and priced the same as purchased energy. Energy from nondepletable energy sources collected on site shall be omitted from the annual energy cost of the Proposed design. The analysis and performance of any nondepletable energy system shall be determined in accordance with accepted engineering practice using approved methods.

806.2.5 Building operation. Building operation shall be simulated for a full calendar year (8,760 hours). Operating schedules shall include hourly profiles for daily operation and shall account for variations between weekdays, weekends, holidays and any seasonal operation. Schedules shall model the time-dependent variations of occupancy, illumination, receptacle loads, thermostat settings, mechanical ventilation, HVAC equipment availability, service hot water usage and any process loads.

806.2.6 Simulated loads. The following systems and loads shall be modeled in determining total building performance: heating systems; cooling systems; fan systems; lighting power; receptacle loads; and process loads that exceed 1.0W/ft^2 ($\text{W}/0.0929 \text{ m}^2$) of floor area of the room or space in which the process loads are located.

> **Exception:** Systems and loads serving required emergency power only.

806.2.7 Service water-heating systems. Service water-heating systems that are other than combined service hot water/space-heating systems shall be omitted from the energy analysis provided all requirements in Section 804 have been met.

806.2.8 Exterior lighting. Exterior lighting systems shall be the same as in the Standard and Proposed designs.

806.3 Determining energy costs for the Proposed design. Building systems and loads shall be simulated in the Proposed design in accordance with Sections 806.3.1 and 806.3.2.

806.3.1 HVAC and service water-heating equipment. All HVAC and service water-heating equipment shall be simulated in the Proposed design using capacities, rated efficiencies and part-load performance data for the proposed equipment as provided by the equipment manufacturer.

806.3.2 Features not documented at time of permit. If any feature of the Proposed design is not included in the building permit application, the energy performance of that feature shall be assumed to be that of the corresponding feature used in the calculations required in Section 806.4.

806.4 Determining energy costs for the Standard design. Sections 806.4.1 through 806.4.7 shall be used in determining the annual energy costs of the Standard design.

806.4.1 Equipment efficiency. The space-heating, space-cooling, service water-heating, and ventilation systems and equipment meet, but not exceed, the minimum efficiency requirements of Sections 803 and 804.

806.4.2 HVAC system capacities. HVAC system capacities in the Standard design shall be established such that no smaller number of unmet heating and cooling load hours and no larger heating and cooling capacity safety factors are provided than in the Proposed design.

806.4.3 Envelope. The performance of the elements of the thermal envelope of the Standard design shall be determined in accordance with the requirements of Section 802.2 as applicable.

806.4.4 Identical characteristics. The heating/cooling system zoning, orientation of each building feature, number of floors and the gross envelope areas of the Standard design shall be the same as those of the Proposed design except as modified by Section 806.4.5 or 806.4.6.

> **Exception:** Permanent fixed or movable external shading devices for windows and glazed doors shall be excluded from the Standard design.

806.4.5 Window area. The window area of the Standard design shall be the same as the Proposed design, or 35 percent of the above-grade wall area, whichever is less, and shall be distributed in a uniform pattern equally over each building façade.

806.4.6 Skylight area. The skylight area of the Standard design shall be the same as the Proposed design, or 3 percent of the gross area of the roof assembly, whichever is less.

806.4.7 Interior lighting. The lighting power for the Standard design shall be the maximum allowed in accordance with Section 805.4. Where the occupancy of the building is not known, the lighting power density shall be 1.5 watts per square foot (16.1 W/m^2).

806.5 Documentation. The energy analysis and supporting documentation shall be prepared by a registered design professional where required by the statutes of the jurisdiction in which the project is to be constructed. The information documenting compliance shall be submitted in accordance with Sections 806.5.1 through 806.5.4.

806.5.1 Annual energy use and associated costs. The annual energy use and costs by energy source of the Standard design and the Proposed design shall be clearly indicated.

806.5.2 Energy-related features. A list of the energy-related features that are included in the proposed design and on which compliance with the provisions of the code are claimed shall be provided by the code official. This list shall include and prominently indicate all features that differ from those set forth in Section 806.4 and used in the energy analysis between the Standard design and the Proposed design.

806.5.3 Input and output report(s). Input and output report(s) from the energy analysis simulation program containing the complete input and output files, as applicable. The output file shall include energy use totals and energy use by energy source and end-use served, total hours that space conditioning loads are not met, and any errors or warning messages generated by the simulation tool as applicable.

806.5.4 Written explanation(s). An explanation of any error or warning messages appearing in the simulation tool output shall be provided in a written, narrative format.

TABLE 802.2(1)

ACCEPTABLE PRACTICE FOR COMMERCIAL BUILDINGS

N
Y

TABLE 802.2(1)
BUILDING ENVELOPE REQUIREMENTS[a through e] - CLIMATE ZONE 10b

WINDOW AND GLAZED DOOR AREA 10 PERCENT OR LESS OF ABOVE-GRADE WALL AREA		
ELEMENT	**CONDITION/VALUE**	
Skylights (U-factor)	0.8	
Slab or below-grade wall (R-value)	R-0	
Windows and glass doors	**SHGC**	**U-factor**
PF < 0.25	Any	Any
0.25 ≤ PF < 0.50	Any	Any
PF ≥ 0.50	Any	Any
Roof assemblies (R-value)	**Insulation between framing**	**Continuous insulation**
All-wood joist/truss	R-19	R-17
Metal joist/truss	R-25	R-18
Concrete slab or deck	NA	R-17
Metal purlin with thermal block	R-30	R-18
Metal purlin without thermal block	X	R-18
Floors over outdoor air or unconditioned space (R-value)	**Insulation between framing**	**Continuous insulation**
All-wood joist/truss	R-19	R-12
Metal joist/truss	R-19	R-13
Concrete slab or deck	NA	R-13

Above-grade walls (R-value)	No framing	Metal framing	Wood framing
Framed			
R-value cavity	NA	R-11	R-11
R-value continuous	NA	R-0	R-0
CMU, ≥ 8 in, with integral insulation			
R-value cavity	NA	R-11	R-11
R-value continuous	R-5	R-0	R-0
Other masonry walls			
R-value cavity	NA	R-11	R-11
R-value continuous	R-5	R-0	R-0

WINDOW AND GLAZED DOOR AREA OVER 10 PERCENT BUT NOT GREATER THAN 25 PERCENT OF ABOVE-GRADE WALL AREA		
ELEMENT	**CONDITION/VALUE**	
Skylights (U-factor)	0.8	
Slab or below-grade wall (R-value)	R-0	
Windows and glass doors	**SHGC**	**U-factor**
PF < 0.25	0.5	0.6
0.25 ≤ PF < 0.50	0.6	0.6
PF ≥ 0.50	0.7	0.6
Roof assemblies (R-value)	**Insulation between framing**	**Continuous insulation**
All-wood joist/truss	R-25	R-19
Metal joist/truss	R-25	R-20
Concrete slab or deck	NA	R-19
Metal purlin with thermal block	R-30	R-20
Metal purlin without thermal block	X	R-20
Floors over outdoor air or unconditioned space (R-value)	**Insulation between framing**	**Continuous insulation**
All-wood joist/truss	R-19	R-12
Metal joist/truss	R-19	R-13
Concrete slab or deck	NA	R-13

Above-grade walls (R-value)	No framing	Metal framing	Wood framing
Framed			
R-value cavity	NA	R-11	R-11
R-value continuous	NA	R-0	R-0
CMU, ≥ 8 in, with integral insulation			
R-value cavity	NA	R-11	R-11
R-value continuous	R-5	R-0	R-0
Other masonry walls			
R-value cavity	NA	R-11	R-11
R-value continuous	R-5	R-0	R-0

(continued)

TABLE 802.2(1)—continued
BUILDING ENVELOPE REQUIREMENTS[a] through [e] - CLIMATE ZONE 10b

WINDOW AND GLAZED DOOR AREA OVER 25 PERCENT BUT NOT GREATER THAN 40 PERCENT OF ABOVE-GRADE WALL AREA

ELEMENT	CONDITION/VALUE		
Skylights (*U*-factor)	0.8		
Slab or below-grade wall (*R*-value)	R-0		
Windows and glass doors	**SHGC**		***U*-factor**
PF < 0.25	0.4		0.5
0.25 ≤ PF < 0.50	0.5		0.5
PF ≥ 0.50	0.6		0.5
Roof assemblies (*R*-value)	**Insulation between framing**		**Continuous insulation**
All-wood joist/truss	R-25		R-19
Metal joist/truss	R-25		R-20
Concrete slab or deck	NA		R-19
Metal purlin with thermal block	R-30		R-20
Metal purlin without thermal block	X		R-20
Floors over outdoor air or unconditioned space (*R*-value)	**Insulation between framing**		**Continuous insulation**
All-wood joist/truss	R-19		R-12
Metal joist/truss	R-19		R-13
Concrete slab or deck	NA		R-13
Above-grade walls (*R*-value)	**No framing**	**Metal framing**	**Wood framing**
Framed			
R-value cavity	NA	R-11	R-11
R-value continuous	NA	R-0	R-0
CMU, ≥ 8 in, with integral insulation			
R-value cavity	NA	R-11	R-11
R-value continuous	R-5	R-0	R-0
Other masonry walls			
R-value cavity	NA	R-11	R-11
R-value continuous	R-5	R-0	R-0

WINDOW AND GLAZED DOOR AREA OVER 40 PERCENT BUT NOT GREATER THAN 50 PERCENT OF ABOVE-GRADE WALL AREA

ELEMENT	CONDITION/VALUE		
Skylights (*U*-factor)	0.8		
Slab or below-grade wall (*R*-value)	R-0		
Windows and glass doors	**SHGC**		***U*-factor**
PF < 0.25	0.3		0.5
0.25 ≤ PF < 0.50	0.4		0.5
PF ≥ 0.50	0.5		0.5
Roof assemblies (*R*-value)	**Insulation between framing**		**Continuous insulation**
All-wood joist/truss	R-25		R-19
Metal joist/truss	R-25		R-20
Concrete slab or deck	NA		R-19
Metal purlin with thermal block	R-30		R-20
Metal purlin without thermal block	R-30		R-20
Floors over outdoor air or unconditioned space (*R*-value)	**Insulation between framing**		**Continuous insulation**
All-wood joist/truss	R-19		R-12
Metal joist/truss	R-19		R-13
Concrete slab or deck	NA		R-13
Above-grade walls (*R*-value)	**No framing**	**Metal framing**	**Wood framing**
Framed			
R-value cavity	NA	R-11	R-11
R-value continuous	NA	R-0	R-0
CMU, ≥ 8 in, with integral insulation			
R-value cavity	NA	R-11	R-11
R-value continuous	R-5	R-0	R-0
Other masonry walls			
R-value cavity	NA	R-11	R-11
R-value continuous	R-5	R-0	R-0

For SI: 1 inch = 25.4 mm
a. "NA" indicates the condition is not applicable.
b. An *R*-value of zero indicates no insulation is required.
c. "Any" indicates any available product will comply.
d. "X" indicates no complying option exists for this condition.

TABLE 802.2(2)

ACCEPTABLE PRACTICE FOR COMMERCIAL BUILDINGS

N
Y

TABLE 802.2(2)
BUILDING ENVELOPE REQUIREMENTS[a through e] - CLIMATE ZONE 11b

WINDOW AND GLAZED DOOR AREA 10 PERCENT OR LESS OF ABOVE-GRADE WALL AREA			
ELEMENT	**CONDITION/VALUE**		
Skylights (*U*-factor)	0.8		
Slab or below-grade wall (*R*-value)	R-0		
Windows and glass doors	**SHGC**		***U*-factor**
PF < 0.25	Any		Any
0.25 ≤ PF < 0.50	Any		Any
PF ≥ 0.50	Any		Any
Roof assemblies (*R*-value)	**Insulation between framing**		**Continuous insulation**
All-wood joist/truss	R-25		R-18
Metal joist/truss	R-25		R-19
Concrete slab or deck	NA		R-18
Metal purlin with thermal block	R-30		R-19
Metal purlin without thermal block	X		R-19
Floors over outdoor air or unconditioned space (*R*-value)	**Insulation between framing**		**Continuous insulation**
All-wood joist/truss	R-19		R-14
Metal joist/truss	R-19		R-15
Concrete slab or deck	NA		R-15
Above-grade walls (*R*-value)	**No framing**	**Metal framing**	**Wood framing**
Framed			
R-value cavity	NA	R-11	R-11
R-value continuous	NA	R-0	R-0
CMU, ≥ 8 in, with integral insulation			
R-value cavity	NA	R-11	R-11
R-value continuous	R-5	R-0	R-0
Other masonry walls			
R-value cavity	NA	R-11	R-11
R-value continuous	R-5	R-0	R-0
WINDOW AND GLAZED DOOR AREA OVER 10 PERCENT BUT NOT GREATER THAN 25 PERCENT OF ABOVE-GRADE WALL AREA			
ELEMENT	**CONDITION/VALUE**		
Skylights (*U*-factor)	0.8		
Slab or below-grade wall (*R*-value)	R-0		
Windows and glass doors	**SHGC**		***U*-factor**
PF < 0.25	0.5		0.6
0.25 ≤ PF < 0.50	0.6		0.6
PF ≥ 0.50	0.7		0.6
Roof assemblies (*R*-value)	**Insulation between framing**		**Continuous insulation**
All-wood joist/truss	R-25		R-19
Metal joist/truss	R-25		R-20
Concrete slab or deck	NA		R-19
Metal purlin with thermal block	R-30		R-20
Metal purlin without thermal block	X		R-20
Floors over outdoor air or unconditioned space (*R*-value)	**Insulation between framing**		**Continuous insulation**
All-wood joist/truss	R-19		R-14
Metal joist/truss	R-19		R-15
Concrete slab or deck	NA		R-15
Above-grade walls (*R*-value)	**No framing**	**Metal framing**	**Wood framing**
Framed			
R-value cavity	NA	R-11	R-11
R-value continuous	NA	R-0	R-0
CMU, ≥ 8 in, with integral insulation			
R-value cavity	NA	R-11	R-11
R-value continuous	R-5	R-0	R-0
Other masonry walls			
R-value cavity	NA	R-11	R-11
R-value continuous	R-5	R-0	R-0

(continued)

TABLE 802.2(2)—continued
BUILDING ENVELOPE REQUIREMENTS[a] through [e] - CLIMATE ZONE 11b

WINDOW AND GLAZED DOOR AREA OVER 25 PERCENT BUT NOT GREATER THAN 40 PERCENT OF ABOVE-GRADE WALL AREA

ELEMENT	CONDITION/VALUE		
Skylights (*U*-factor)	0.8		
Slab or below-grade wall (*R*-value)	R-8		
Windows and glass doors	**SHGC**		**U-factor**
PF < 0.25	0.4		0.5
0.25 ≤ PF < 0.50	0.5		0.5
PF ≥ 0.50	0.6		0.5
Roof assemblies (*R*-value)	**Insulation between framing**		**Continuous insulation**
All-wood joist/truss	R-30		R-23
Metal joist/truss	R-30		R-24
Concrete slab or deck	NA		R-23
Metal purlin with thermal block	X		R-24
Metal purlin without thermal block	X		R-24
Floors over outdoor air or unconditioned space (*R*-value)	**Insulation between framing**		**Continuous insulation**
All-wood joist/truss	R-19		R-14
Metal joist/truss	R-19		R-15
Concrete slab or deck	NA		R-15
Above-grade walls (*R*-value)	**No framing**	**Metal framing**	**Wood framing**
Framed			
R-value cavity	NA	R-11	R-11
R-value continuous	NA	R-0	R-0
CMU, ≥ 8 in, with integral insulation			
R-value cavity	NA	R-11	R-11
R-value continuous	R-5	R-0	R-0
Other masonry walls			
R-value cavity	NA	R-11	R-11
R-value continuous	R-5	R-0	R-0

WINDOW AND GLAZED DOOR AREA OVER 40 PERCENT BUT NOT GREATER THAN 50 PERCENT OF ABOVE-GRADE WALL AREA

ELEMENT	CONDITION/VALUE		
Skylights (*U*-factor)	0.8		
Slab or below-grade wall (*R*-value)	R-8		
Windows and glass doors	**SHGC**		**U-factor**
PF < 0.25	0.3		0.5
0.25 ≤ PF < 0.50	0.4		0.5
PF ≥ 0.50	0.5		0.5
Roof assemblies (*R*-value)	**Insulation between framing**		**Continuous insulation**
All-wood joist/truss	R-30		R-23
Metal joist/truss	R-30		R-24
Concrete slab or deck	NA		R-23
Metal purlin with thermal block	R-30		R-24
Metal purlin without thermal block	R-38		R-24
Floors over outdoor air or unconditioned space (*R*-value)	**Insulation between framing**		**Continuous insulation**
All-wood joist/truss	R-19		R-14
Metal joist/truss	R-19		R-15
Concrete slab or deck	NA		R-15
Above-grade walls (*R*-value)	**No framing**	**Metal framing**	**Wood framing**
Framed			
R-value cavity	NA	R-13	R-11
R-value continuous	NA	R-3	R-0
CMU, ≥ 8 in, with integral insulation			
R-value cavity	NA	R-11	R-11
R-value continuous	R-5	R-0	R-0
Other masonry walls			
R-value cavity	NA	R-11	R-11
R-value continuous	R-5	R-0	R-0

For SI: 1 inch = 25.4 mm

a. "NA" indicates the condition is not applicable.

b. An *R*-value of zero indicates no insulation is required.

c. "Any" indicates any available product will comply.

d. "X" indicates no complying option exists for this condition.

TABLE 802.2(3)

ACCEPTABLE PRACTICE FOR COMMERCIAL BUILDINGS

N
Y

TABLE 802.2(3)
BUILDING ENVELOPE REQUIREMENTSa through e **- CLIMATE ZONE 12b**

WINDOW AND GLAZED DOOR AREA 10 PERCENT OR LESS OF ABOVE-GRADE WALL AREA

ELEMENT	CONDITION/VALUE		
Skylights (*U*-factor)	0.8		
Slab or below-grade wall (*R*-value)	R-0		
Windows and glass doors	**SHGC**		***U*-factor**
PF < 0.25	Any		Any
0.25 ≤ PF < 0.50	Any		Any
PF ≥ 0.50	Any		Any
Roof assemblies (*R*-value)	**Insulation between framing**		**Continuous insulation**
All-wood joist/truss	R-19		R-16
Metal joist/truss	R-25		R-17
Concrete slab or deck	NA		R-16
Metal purlin with thermal block	R-25		R-17
Metal purlin without thermal block	X		R-17
Floors over outdoor air or unconditioned space (*R*-value)	**Insulation between framing**		**Continuous insulation**
All-wood joist/truss	R-19		R-15
Metal joist/truss	R-19		R-16
Concrete slab or deck	NA		R-16
Above-grade walls (*R*-value)	**No framing**	**Metal framing**	**Wood framing**
Framed			
R-value cavity	NA	R-11	R-11
R-value continuous	NA	R-0	R-0
CMU, ≥ 8 in, with integral insulation			
R-value cavity	NA	R-11	R-11
R-value continuous	R-5	R-0	R-0
Other masonry walls			
R-value cavity	NA	R-11	R-11
R-value continuous	R-5	R-0	R-0

WINDOW AND GLAZED DOOR AREA OVER 10 PERCENT BUT NOT GREATER THAN 25 PERCENT OF ABOVE-GRADE WALL AREA

ELEMENT	CONDITION/VALUE		
Skylights (*U*-factor)	0.8		
Slab or below-grade wall (*R*-value)	R-0		
Windows and glass doors	**SHGC**		***U*-factor**
PF < 0.25	0.5		0.6
0.25 ≤ PF < 0.50	0.6		0.6
PF ≥ 0.50	0.7		0.6
Roof assemblies (*R*-value)	**Insulation between framing**		**Continuous insulation**
All-wood joist/truss	R-25		R-19
Metal joist/truss	R-25		R-20
Concrete slab or deck	NA		R-19
Metal purlin with thermal block	R-30		R-20
Metal purlin without thermal block	X		R-20
Floors over outdoor air or unconditioned space (*R*-value)	**Insulation between framing**		**Continuous insulation**
All-wood joist/truss	R-19		R-15
Metal joist/truss	R-19		R-16
Concrete slab or deck	NA		R-16
Above-grade walls (*R*-value)	**No framing**	**Metal framing**	**Wood framing**
Framed			
R-value cavity	NA	R-11	R-11
R-value continuous	NA	R-0	R-0
CMU, ≥ 8 in, with integral insulation			
R-value cavity	NA	R-11	R-11
R-value continuous	R-5	R-0	R-0
Other masonry walls			
R-value cavity	NA	R-11	R-11
R-value continuous	R-5	R-0	R-0

(continued)

TABLE 802.2(3)—continued
BUILDING ENVELOPE REQUIREMENTS[a] through [e] - CLIMATE ZONE 12b

WINDOW AND GLAZED DOOR AREA OVER 25 PERCENT BUT NOT GREATER THAN 40 PERCENT OF ABOVE-GRADE WALL AREA

ELEMENT	CONDITION/VALUE		
Skylights (U-factor)	0.8		
Slab or below-grade wall (R-value)	R-8		
Windows and glass doors	**SHGC**	**U-factor**	
PF < 0.25	0.4	0.5	
0.25 ≤ PF < 0.50	0.5	0.5	
PF ≥ 0.50	0.6	0.5	
Roof assemblies (R-value)	**Insulation between framing**	**Continuous insulation**	
All-wood joist/truss	R-30	R-23	
Metal joist/truss	R-30	R-24	
Concrete slab or deck	NA	R-23	
Metal purlin with thermal block	X	R-24	
Metal purlin without thermal block	X	R-24	
Floors over outdoor air or unconditioned space (R-value)	**Insulation between framing**	**Continuous insulation**	
All-wood joist/truss	R-19	R-15	
Metal joist/truss	R-19	R-16	
Concrete slab or deck	NA	R-16	
Above-grade walls (R-value)	**No framing**	**Metal framing**	**Wood framing**
Framed			
R-value cavity	NA	R-11	R-11
R-value continuous	NA	R-0	R-0
CMU, ≥ 8 in, with integral insulation			
R-value cavity	NA	R-11	R-11
R-value continuous	R-5	R-0	R-0
Other masonry walls			
R-value cavity	NA	R-11	R-11
R-value continuous	R-5	R-0	R-0

WINDOW AND GLAZED DOOR AREA OVER 40 PERCENT BUT NOT GREATER THAN 50 PERCENT OF ABOVE-GRADE WALL AREA

ELEMENT	CONDITION/VALUE		
Skylights (U-factor)	0.8		
Slab or below-grade wall (R-value)	R-8		
Windows and glass doors	**SHGC**	**U-factor**	
PF < 0.25	0.3	0.5	
0.25 ≤ PF < 0.50	0.4	0.5	
PF ≥ 0.50	0.5	0.5	
Roof assemblies (R-value)	**Insulation between framing**	**Continuous insulation**	
All-wood joist/truss	R-30	R-23	
Metal joist/truss	R-30	R-24	
Concrete slab or deck	NA	R-23	
Metal purlin with thermal block	R-38	R-24	
Metal purlin without thermal block	R-49	R-24	
Floors over outdoor air or unconditioned space (R-value)	**Insulation between framing**	**Continuous insulation**	
All-wood joist/truss	R-19	R-15	
Metal joist/truss	R-19	R-16	
Concrete slab or deck	NA	R-16	
Above-grade walls (R-value)	**No framing**	**Metal framing**	**Wood framing**
Framed			
R-value cavity	NA	R-13	R-13
R-value continuous	NA	R-3	R-0
CMU, ≥ 8 in, with integral insulation			
R-value cavity	NA	R-11	R-11
R-value continuous	R-5	R-0	R-0
Other masonry walls			
R-value cavity	NA	R-11	R-11
R-value continuous	R-5	R-0	R-0

For SI: 1 inch = 25.4 mm

a. "NA" indicates the condition is not applicable.
b. An R-value of zero indicates no insulation is required.
c. "Any" indicates any available product will comply.
d. "X" indicates no complying option exists for this condition.

TABLE 802.2(4)   ACCEPTABLE PRACTICE FOR COMMERCIAL BUILDINGS

N
Y

TABLE 802.2(4)
BUILDING ENVELOPE REQUIREMENTSa through e - CLIMATE ZONE 13a

WINDOW AND GLAZED DOOR AREA 10 PERCENT OR LESS OF ABOVE-GRADE WALL AREA		
ELEMENT	**CONDITION/VALUE**	
Skylights (*U*-factor)	0.8	
Slab or below-grade wall (*R*-value)	R-0	

Windows and glass doors	SHGC	*U*-factor
PF < 0.25	Any	0.7
0.25 ≤ PF < 0.50	Any	0.7
PF ≥ 0.50	Any	0.7

Roof assemblies (*R*-value)	Insulation between framing	Continuous insulation
All-wood joist/truss	R-19	R-14
Metal joist/truss	R-19	R-15
Concrete slab or deck	NA	R-14
Metal purlin with thermal block	R-25	R-15
Metal purlin without thermal block	X	R-15

Floors over outdoor air or unconditioned space (*R*-value)	Insulation between framing	Continuous insulation
All-wood joist/truss	R-19	R-16
Metal joist/truss	R-25	R-17
Concrete slab or deck	NA	R-17

Above-grade walls (*R*-value)	No framing	Metal framing	Wood framing
Framed			
R-value cavity	NA	R-13	R-11
R-value continuous	NA	R-0	R-0
CMU, ≥ 8 in, with integral insulation			
R-value cavity	NA	R-11	R-11
R-value continuous	R-5	R-0	R-0
Other masonry walls			
R-value cavity	NA	R-11	R-11
R-value continuous	R-5	R-0	R-0

WINDOW AND GLAZED DOOR AREA OVER 10 PERCENT BUT NOT GREATER THAN 25 PERCENT OF ABOVE-GRADE WALL AREA		
ELEMENT	**CONDITION/VALUE**	
Skylights (*U*-factor)	0.8	
Slab or below-grade wall (*R*-value)	R-0	

Windows and glass doors	SHGC	*U*-factor
PF < 0.25	0.6	0.6
0.25 ≤ PF < 0.50	0.7	0.6
PF ≥ 0.50	Any	0.6

Roof assemblies (*R*-value)	Insulation between framing	Continuous insulation
All-wood joist/truss	R-25	R-19
Metal joist/truss	R-25	R-20
Concrete slab or deck	NA	R-19
Metal purlin with thermal block	R-30	R-20
Metal purlin without thermal block	X	R-20

Floors over outdoor air or unconditioned space (*R*-value)	Insulation between framing	Continuous insulation
All-wood joist/truss	R-19	R-16
Metal joist/truss	R-25	R-17
Concrete slab or deck	NA	R-17

Above-grade walls (*R*-value)	No framing	Metal framing	Wood framing
Framed			
R-value cavity	NA	R-13	R-11
R-value continuous	NA	R-0	R-0
CMU, ≥ 8 in, with integral insulation			
R-value cavity	NA	R-11	R-11
R-value continuous	R-5	R-0	R-0
Other masonry walls			
R-value cavity	NA	R-11	R-11
R-value continuous	R-5	R-0	R-0

(continued)

TABLE 802.2(4)—continued
BUILDING ENVELOPE REQUIREMENTS[a through e] - CLIMATE ZONE 13a

WINDOW AND GLAZED DOOR AREA OVER 25 PERCENT BUT NOT GREATER THAN 40 PERCENT OF ABOVE-GRADE WALL AREA		
ELEMENT	**CONDITION/VALUE**	
Skylights (U-factor)	0.8	
Slab or below-grade wall (R-value)	R-8	
Windows and glass doors	SHGC	U-factor
PF < 0.25	0.5	0.5
0.25 ≤ PF < 0.50	0.6	0.5
PF ≥ 0.50	0.7	0.5
Roof assemblies (R-value)	Insulation between framing	Continuous insulation
All-wood joist/truss	R-30	R-23
Metal joist/truss	R-30	R-24
Concrete slab or deck	NA	R-23
Metal purlin with thermal block	X	R-24
Metal purlin without thermal block	X	R-24
Floors over outdoor air or unconditioned space (R-value)	Insulation between framing	Continuous insulation
All-wood joist/truss	R-19	R-16
Metal joist/truss	R-25	R-17
Concrete slab or deck	NA	R-17

Above-grade walls (R-value)	No framing	Metal framing	Wood framing
Framed			
R-value cavity	NA	R-13	R-11
R-value continuous	NA	R-0	R-0
CMU, ≥ 8 in, with integral insulation			
R-value cavity	NA	R-11	R-11
R-value continuous	R-5	R-0	R-0
Other masonry walls			
R-value cavity	NA	R-11	R-11
R-value continuous	R-5	R-0	R-0

WINDOW AND GLAZED DOOR AREA OVER 40 PERCENT BUT NOT GREATER THAN 50 PERCENT OF ABOVE-GRADE WALL AREA		
ELEMENT	**CONDITION/VALUE**	
Skylights (U-factor)	0.8	
Slab or below-grade wall (R-value)	R-8	
Windows and glass doors	SHGC	U-factor
PF < 0.25	0.4	0.4
0.25 ≤ PF < 0.50	0.5	0.4
PF ≥ 0.50	0.7	0.4
Roof assemblies (R-value)	Insulation between framing	Continuous insulation
All-wood joist/truss	R-30	R-23
Metal joist/truss	R-30	R-24
Concrete slab or deck	NA	R-23
Metal purlin with thermal block	R-30	R-24
Metal purlin without thermal block	R-38	R-24
Floors over outdoor air or unconditioned space (R-value)	Insulation between framing	Continuous insulation
All-wood joist/truss	R-19	R-16
Metal joist/truss	R-25	R-17
Concrete slab or deck	NA	R-17

Above-grade walls (R-value)	No framing	Metal framing	Wood framing
Framed			
R-value cavity	NA	R-13	R-11
R-value continuous	NA	R-0	R-0
CMU, ≥ 8 in, with integral insulation			
R-value cavity	NA	R-11	R-11
R-value continuous	R-5	R-0	R-0
Other masonry walls			
R-value cavity	NA	R-11	R-11
R-value continuous	R-5	R-0	R-0

For SI: 1 inch = 25.4 mm

a. "NA" indicates the condition is not applicable.
b. An R-value of zero indicates no insulation is required.
c. "Any" indicates any available product will comply.
d. "X" indicates no complying option exists for this condition.

TABLE 802.2(5)

ACCEPTABLE PRACTICE FOR COMMERCIAL BUILDINGS

N
Y

TABLE 802.2(5)
BUILDING ENVELOPE REQUIREMENTS[a] through [e] - CLIMATE ZONE 14a

WINDOW AND GLAZED DOOR AREA 10 PERCENT OR LESS OF ABOVE-GRADE WALL AREA		
ELEMENT	**CONDITION/VALUE**	
Skylights (U-factor)	0.8	
Slab or below-grade wall (R-value)	R-0	
Windows and glass doors	**SHGC**	**U-factor**
PF < 0.25	Any	0.7
0.25 ≤ PF < 0.50	Any	0.7
PF ≥ 0.50	Any	0.7
Roof assemblies (R-value)	**Insulation between framing**	**Continuous insulation**
All-wood joist/truss	R-19	R-17
Metal joist/truss	R-25	R-18
Concrete slab or deck	NA	R-17
Metal purlin with thermal block	R-30	R-18
Metal purlin without thermal block	X	R-18
Floors over outdoor air or unconditioned space (R-value)	**Insulation between framing**	**Continuous insulation**
All-wood joist/truss	R-25	R-18
Metal joist/truss	R-25	R-19
Concrete slab or deck	NA	R-19

Above-grade walls (R-value)	**No framing**	**Metal framing**	**Wood framing**
Framed			
R-value cavity	NA	R-13	R-11
R-value continuous	NA	R-3	R-0
CMU, ≥ 8 in, with integral insulation			
R-value cavity	NA	R-11	R-11
R-value continuous	R-5	R-0	R-0
Other masonry walls			
R-value cavity	NA	R-11	R-11
R-value continuous	R-5	R-0	R-0

WINDOW AND GLAZED DOOR AREA OVER 10 PERCENT BUT NOT GREATER THAN 25 PERCENT OF ABOVE-GRADE WALL AREA		
ELEMENT	**CONDITION/VALUE**	
Skylights (U-factor)	0.8	
Slab or below-grade wall (R-value)	R-8	
Windows and glass doors	**SHGC**	**U-factor**
PF < 0.25	0.5	0.6
0.25 ≤ PF < 0.50	0.6	0.6
PF ≥ 0.50	0.7	0.6
Roof assemblies (R-value)	**Insulation between framing**	**Continuous insulation**
All-wood joist/truss	R-25	R-19
Metal joist/truss	R-25	R-20
Concrete slab or deck	NA	R-19
Metal purlin with thermal block	R-30	R-20
Metal purlin without thermal block	X	R-20
Floors over outdoor air or unconditioned space (R-value)	**Insulation between framing**	**Continuous insulation**
All-wood joist/truss	R-25	R-18
Metal joist/truss	R-25	R-19
Concrete slab or deck	NA	R-19

Above-grade walls (R-value)	**No framing**	**Metal framing**	**Wood framing**
Framed			
R-value cavity	NA	R-13	R-11
R-value continuous	NA	R-3	R-0
CMU, ≥ 8 in, with integral insulation			
R-value cavity	NA	R-11	R-11
R-value continuous	R-5	R-0	R-0
Other masonry walls			
R-value cavity	NA	R-11	R-11
R-value continuous	R-5	R-0	R-0

(continued)

TABLE 802.2(5)—continued
BUILDING ENVELOPE REQUIREMENTS[a] through [e] - CLIMATE ZONE 14a

WINDOW AND GLAZED DOOR AREA OVER 25 PERCENT BUT NOT GREATER THAN 40 PERCENT OF ABOVE-GRADE WALL AREA

ELEMENT	CONDITION/VALUE		
Skylights (*U*-factor)	0.8		
Slab or below-grade wall (*R*-value)	R-8		
Windows and glass doors	**SHGC**		***U*-factor**
PF < 0.25	0.4		0.5
0.25 ≤ PF < 0.50	0.5		0.5
PF ≥ 0.50	0.6		0.5
Roof assemblies (*R*-value)	**Insulation between framing**		**Continuous insulation**
All-wood joist/truss	R-30		R-23
Metal joist/truss	R-30		R-24
Concrete slab or deck	NA		R-23
Metal purlin with thermal block	X		R-24
Metal purlin without thermal block	X		R-24
Floors over outdoor air or unconditioned space (*R*-value)	**Insulation between framing**		**Continuous insulation**
All-wood joist/truss	R-25		R-18
Metal joist/truss	R-25		R-19
Concrete slab or deck	NA		R-19
Above-grade walls (*R*-value)	**No framing**	**Metal framing**	**Wood framing**
Framed			
R-value cavity	NA	R-13	R-11
R-value continuous	NA	R-3	R-0
CMU, ≥ 8 in, with integral insulation			
R-value cavity	NA	R-11	R-11
R-value continuous	R-5	R-0	R-0
Other masonry walls			
R-value cavity	NA	R-11	R-11
R-value continuous	R-5	R-0	R-0

WINDOW AND GLAZED DOOR AREA OVER 40 PERCENT BUT NOT GREATER THAN 50 PERCENT OF ABOVE-GRADE WALL AREA

ELEMENT	CONDITION/VALUE		
Skylights (*U*-factor)	0.8		
Slab or below-grade wall (*R*-value)	R-8		
Windows and glass doors	**SHGC**		***U*-factor**
PF < 0.25	0.4		0.4
0.25 ≤ PF < 0.50	0.5		0.4
PF ≥ 0.50	0.6		0.4
Roof assemblies (*R*-value)	**Insulation between framing**		**Continuous insulation**
All-wood joist/truss	R-30		R-23
Metal joist/truss	R-30		R-24
Concrete slab or deck	NA		R-23
Metal purlin with thermal block	R-38		R-24
Metal purlin without thermal block	R-38		R-24
Floors over outdoor air or unconditioned space (*R*-value)	**Insulation between framing**		**Continuous insulation**
All-wood joist/truss	R-25		R-18
Metal joist/truss	R-25		R-19
Concrete slab or deck	NA		R-19
Above-grade walls (*R*-value)	**No framing**	**Metal framing**	**Wood framing**
Framed			
R-value cavity	NA	R-13	R-11
R-value continuous	NA	R-3	R-0
CMU, ≥ 8 in, with integral insulation			
R-value cavity	NA	R-11	R-11
R-value continuous	R-5	R-0	R-0
Other masonry walls			
R-value cavity	NA	R-11	R-11
R-value continuous	R-5	R-0	R-0

For SI: 1 inch = 25.4 mm
a. "NA" indicates the condition is not applicable.
b. An *R*-value of zero indicates no insulation is required.
c. "Any" indicates any available product will comply.
d. "X" indicates no complying option exists for this condition.

TABLE 802.2(6)

ACCEPTABLE PRACTICE FOR COMMERCIAL BUILDINGS

N
Y

TABLE 802.2(6)
BUILDING ENVELOPE REQUIREMENTS[a through e] **- CLIMATE ZONE 15**

WINDOW AND GLAZED DOOR AREA 10 PERCENT OR LESS OF ABOVE-GRADE WALL AREA			
ELEMENT	CONDITION/VALUE		
Skylights (*U*-factor)	0.6		
Slab or below-grade wall (*R*-value)	R-0		
Windows and glass doors	SHGC		*U*-factor
PF < 0.25	Any		0.7
0.25 ≤ PF < 0.50	Any		0.7
PF ≥ 0.50	Any		0.7
Roof assemblies (*R*-value)	Insulation between framing		Continuous insulation
All-wood joist/truss	R-25		R-19
Metal joist/truss	R-25		R-20
Concrete slab or deck	NA		R-19
Metal purlin with thermal block	R-30		R-20
Metal purlin without thermal block	X		R-20
Floors over outdoor air or unconditioned space (*R*-value)	Insulation between framing		Continuous insulation
All-wood joist/truss	R-25		R-22
Metal joist/truss	R-30		R-23
Concrete slab or deck	NA		R-22
Above-grade walls (*R*-value)	No framing	Metal framing	Wood framing
Framed			
R-value cavity	NA	R-13	R-11
R-value continuous	NA	R-3	R-0
CMU, ≥ 8 in, with integral insulation			
R-value cavity	NA	R-11	R-11
R-value continuous	R-5	R-0	R-0
Other masonry walls			
R-value cavity	NA	R-11	R-11
R-value continuous	R-5	R-0	R-0

WINDOW AND GLAZED DOOR AREA OVER 10 PERCENT BUT NOT GREATER THAN 25 PERCENT OF ABOVE-GRADE WALL AREA			
ELEMENT	CONDITION/VALUE		
Skylights (*U*-factor)	0.6		
Slab or below-grade wall (*R*-value)	R-8		
Windows and glass doors	SHGC		*U*-factor
PF < 0.25	0.5		0.5
0.25 ≤ PF < 0.50	0.6		0.5
PF ≥ 0.50	0.7		0.5
Roof assemblies (*R*-value)	Insulation between framing		Continuous insulation
All-wood joist/truss	R-25		R-19
Metal joist/truss	R-25		R-20
Concrete slab or deck	NA		R-19
Metal purlin with thermal block	R-30		R-20
Metal purlin without thermal block	X		R-20
Floors over outdoor air or unconditioned space (*R*-value)	Insulation between framing		Continuous insulation
All-wood joist/truss	R-25		R-22
Metal joist/truss	R-30		R-23
Concrete slab or deck	NA		R-22
Above-grade walls (*R*-value)	No framing	Metal framing	Wood framing
Framed			
R-value cavity	NA	R-13	R-11
R-value continuous	NA	R-3	R-0
CMU, ≥ 8 in, with integral insulation			
R-value cavity	NA	R-11	R-11
R-value continuous	R-5	R-0	R-0
Other masonry walls			
R-value cavity	NA	R-11	R-11
R-value continuous	R-5	R-0	R-0

(continued)

TABLE 802.2(6)—continued
BUILDING ENVELOPE REQUIREMENTS[a through e] - CLIMATE ZONE 15

WINDOW AND GLAZED DOOR AREA OVER 25 PERCENT BUT NOT GREATER THAN 40 PERCENT OF ABOVE-GRADE WALL AREA		
ELEMENT	**CONDITION/VALUE**	
Skylights (U-factor)	0.6	
Slab or below-grade wall (R-value)	R-8	

Windows and glass doors	SHGC	U-factor
PF < 0.25	0.5	0.4
0.25 ≤ PF < 0.50	0.6	0.4
PF ≥ 0.50	0.7	0.4

Roof assemblies (R-value)	Insulation between framing	Continuous insulation
All-wood joist/truss	R-30	R-23
Metal joist/truss	R-30	R-24
Concrete slab or deck	NA	R-23
Metal purlin with thermal block	X	R-24
Metal purlin without thermal block	X	R-24

Floors over outdoor air or unconditioned space (R-value)	Insulation between framing	Continuous insulation
All-wood joist/truss	R-25	R-22
Metal joist/truss	R-30	R-23
Concrete slab or deck	NA	R-22

Above-grade walls (R-value)	No framing	Metal framing	Wood framing
Framed			
R-value cavity	NA	R-13	R-11
R-value continuous	NA	R-3	R-0
CMU, ≥ 8 in, with integral insulation			
R-value cavity	NA	R-11	R-11
R-value continuous	R-5	R-0	R-0
Other masonry walls			
R-value cavity	NA	R-13	R-11
R-value continuous	R-6	R-0	R-0

WINDOW AND GLAZED DOOR AREA OVER 40 PERCENT BUT NOT GREATER THAN 50 PERCENT OF ABOVE-GRADE WALL AREA		
ELEMENT	**CONDITION/VALUE**	
Skylights (U-factor)	0.6	
Slab or below-grade wall (R-value)	R-8	

Windows and glass doors	SHGC	U-factor
PF < 0.25	0.4	0.4
0.25 ≤ PF < 0.50	0.5	0.4
PF ≥ 0.50	0.7	0.4

Roof assemblies (R-value)	Insulation between framing	Continuous insulation
All-wood joist/truss	R-30	R-23
Metal joist/truss	R-30	R-24
Concrete slab or deck	NA	R-23
Metal purlin with thermal block	R-38	R-24
Metal purlin without thermal block	X	R-24

Floors over outdoor air or unconditioned space (R-value)	Insulation between framing	Continuous insulation
All-wood joist/truss	R-25	R-22
Metal joist/truss	R-30	R-23
Concrete slab or deck	NA	R-22

Above-grade walls (R-value)	No framing	Metal framing	Wood framing
Framed			
R-value cavity	NA	R-13	R-13
R-value continuous	NA	R-7	R-4
CMU, ≥ 8 in, with integral insulation			
R-value cavity	NA	R-13	R-11
R-value continuous	R-5	R-0	R-0
Other masonry walls			
R-value cavity	NA	R-13	R-11
R-value continuous	R-6	R-3	R-0

For SI: 1 inch = 25.4 mm

a. "NA" indicates the condition is not applicable.

b. An R-value of zero indicates no insulation is required.

c. "Any" indicates any available product will comply.

d. "X" indicates no complying option exists for this condition.

TABLE 802.2(7)

ACCEPTABLE PRACTICE FOR COMMERCIAL BUILDINGS

N
Y

TABLE 802.2(7)
BUILDING ENVELOPE REQUIREMENTS[a through e] - CLIMATE ZONE 16

WINDOW AND GLAZED DOOR AREA 10 PERCENT OR LESS OF ABOVE-GRADE WALL AREA		
ELEMENT	**CONDITION/VALUE**	
Skylights (*U*-factor)	0.6	
Slab or below-grade wall (*R*-value)	R-8	
Windows and glass doors	**SHGC**	***U*-factor**
PF < 0.25	0.7	0.6
0.25 ≤ PF < 0.50	Any	0.6
PF ≥ 0.50	Any	0.6
Roof assemblies (*R*-value)	**Insulation between framing**	**Continuous insulation**
All-wood joist/truss	R-25	R-19
Metal joist/truss	R-25	R-20
Concrete slab or deck	NA	R-19
Metal purlin with thermal block	R-30	R-20
Metal purlin without thermal block	X	R-20
Floors over outdoor air or unconditioned space (*R*-value)	**Insulation between framing**	**Continuous insulation**
All-wood joist/truss	R-25	R-22
Metal joist/truss	R-30	R-23
Concrete slab or deck	NA	R-22

Above-grade walls (*R*-value)	**No framing**	**Metal framing**	**Wood framing**
Framed			
R-value cavity	NA	R-13	R-11
R-value continuous	NA	R-3	R-0
CMU, ≥ 8 in, with integral insulation			
R-value cavity	NA	R-11	R-11
R-value continuous	R-5	R-0	R-0
Other masonry walls			
R-value cavity	NA	R-11	R-11
R-value continuous	R-5	R-0	R-0

WINDOW AND GLAZED DOOR AREA OVER 10 PERCENT BUT NOT GREATER THAN 25 PERCENT OF ABOVE-GRADE WALL AREA		
ELEMENT	**CONDITION/VALUE**	
Skylights (*U*-factor)	0.6	
Slab or below-grade wall (*R*-value)	R-8	
Windows and glass doors	**SHGC**	***U*-factor**
PF < 0.25	0.7	0.5
0.25 ≤ PF < 0.50	Any	0.5
PF ≥ 0.50	Any	0.5
Roof assemblies (*R*-value)	**Insulation between framing**	**Continuous insulation**
All-wood joist/truss	R-30	R-23
Metal joist/truss	R-30	R-24
Concrete slab or deck	NA	R-23
Metal purlin with thermal block	X	R-24
Metal purlin without thermal block	X	R-24
Floors over outdoor air or unconditioned space (*R*-value)	**Insulation between framing**	**Continuous insulation**
All-wood joist/truss	R-25	R-22
Metal joist/truss	R-30	R-23
Concrete slab or deck	NA	R-22

Above-grade walls (*R*-value)	**No framing**	**Metal framing**	**Wood framing**
Framed			
R-value cavity	NA	R-13	R-11
R-value continuous	NA	R-3	R-0
CMU, ≥ 8 in, with integral insulation			
R-value cavity	NA	R-11	R-11
R-value continuous	R-5	R-0	R-0
Other masonry walls			
R-value cavity	NA	R-13	R-11
R-value continuous	R-9	R-3	R-0

(continued)

TABLE 802.2(7)—continued
BUILDING ENVELOPE REQUIREMENTS[a through e] - CLIMATE ZONE 16

WINDOW AND GLAZED DOOR AREA OVER 25 PERCENT BUT NOT GREATER THAN 40 PERCENT OF ABOVE-GRADE WALL AREA

ELEMENT	CONDITION/VALUE		
Skylights (U-factor)	0.6		
Slab or below-grade wall (R-value)	R-8		
Windows and glass doors	**SHGC**		**U-factor**
PF < 0.25	0.5		0.4
0.25 ≤ PF < 0.50	0.6		0.4
PF ≥ 0.50	0.7		0.4
Roof assemblies (R-value)	**Insulation between framing**		**Continuous insulation**
All-wood joist/truss	R-30		R-23
Metal joist/truss	R-30		R-24
Concrete slab or deck	NA		R-23
Metal purlin with thermal block	X		R-24
Metal purlin without thermal block	X		R-24
Floors over outdoor air or unconditioned space (R-value)	**Insulation between framing**		**Continuous insulation**
All-wood joist/truss	R-25		R-22
Metal joist/truss	R-30		R-23
Concrete slab or deck	NA		R-22
Above-grade walls (R-value)	**No framing**	**Metal framing**	**Wood framing**
Framed			
R-value cavity	NA	R-13	R-13
R-value continuous	NA	R-3	R-0
CMU, ≥ 8 in, with integral insulation			
R-value cavity	NA	R-13	R-11
R-value continuous	R-6	R-0	R-0
Other masonry walls			
R-value cavity	NA	R-13	R-13
R-value continuous	R-9	R-3	R-0

WINDOW AND GLAZED DOOR AREA OVER 40 PERCENT BUT NOT GREATER THAN 50 PERCENT OF ABOVE-GRADE WALL AREA

ELEMENT	CONDITION/VALUE		
Skylights (U-factor)	0.6		
Slab or below-grade wall (R-value)	R-8		
Windows and glass doors	**SHGC**		**U-factor**
PF < 0.25	0.4		0.4
0.25 ≤ PF < 0.50	0.5		0.4
PF ≥ 0.50	0.7		0.4
Roof assemblies (R-value)	**Insulation between framing**		**Continuous insulation**
All-wood joist/truss	R-30		R-23
Metal joist/truss	R-30		R-24
Concrete slab or deck	NA		R-23
Metal purlin with thermal block	R-38		R-24
Metal purlin without thermal block	X		R-24
Floors over outdoor air or unconditioned space (R-value)	**Insulation between framing**		**Continuous insulation**
All-wood joist/truss	R-25		R-22
Metal joist/truss	R-30		R-23
Concrete slab or deck	NA		R-22
Above-grade walls (R-value)	**No framing**	**Metal framing**	**Wood framing**
Framed			
R-value cavity	NA	R-13	R-13
R-value continuous	NA	R-14	R-7
CMU, ≥ 8 in, with integral insulation			
R-value cavity	NA	R-13	R-13
R-value continuous	R-10	R-3	R-0
Other masonry walls			
R-value cavity	NA	R-13	R-13
R-value continuous	R-9	R-3	R-3

For SI: 1 inch = 25.4 mm
a. "NA" indicates the condition is not applicable.
b. An R-value of zero indicates no insulation is required.
c. "Any" indicates any available product will comply.
d. "X" indicates no complying option exists for this condition.

CHAPTER 9
REFERENCED STANDARDS

This chapter lists the standards that are referenced in various sections of this document. The standards are listed herein by the promulgating agency of the standard, the standard identification, the effective date and title, and the section or sections of this document that reference the standard. The application of the referenced standards shall be as specified in Section 107.

AAMA

American Architectural Manufacturers Association
1827 Walden Office Square, Suite 104
Schaumburg, IL 60173-4628

Standard reference number	Title	Referenced in code section number
101/I.S.2—97	Voluntary Specifications for Aluminum, Vinyl (PVC) and Wood Windows and Glass Doors	Table 502.1.4.1, 601.3.2.2, 802.3.1

AMCA

Air Movement and Control Association International
30 West University Drive
Arlington Heights, IL 60004-1806

Standard reference number	Title	Referenced in code section number
AMCA 500-89	Test Methods for Louvers, Dampers, and Shutters	802.3.3

ANSI

American National Standards Institute
11 West 42nd Street
New York, NY 10036

Standard reference number	Title	Referenced in code section number
Z21.10.3—98	Gas Water Heaters, Volume III, Circulating Tank, Instantaneous and Large Automatic Storage-Type Heaters	Table 504.2
Z21.13—91	Gas-Fired Low-Pressure Steam and Hot Water Boilers—with 1993 and 1994 Addenda	Table 803.2.2(5)
Z21.47—93	Gas-Fired Central Furnaces (Except Direct Vent and Separated Combustion System Furnaces) — with Addendum Z21.47a-1995 and Z21.47b-1997	Table 803.2.2(4)
Z21.56—98	Gas-Fired Pool Heaters	Table 504.2
Z83.8—96	Gas-Fired Duct Furnaces—with Addendum Z83.8a-1997	Table 803.2.2(4)
Z83.9—96	Gas Unit Heaters	Table 803.2.2(4)
Z21.50—96	Vented Gas Fireplaces	102.7.3
Z21.60—96	Decorative Gas Appliances for Installation in Solid-Fuel-Burning Fireplaces	102.7.2

ARI

Air Conditioning and Refrigeration Institute
4301 North Fairfax Drive
Suite 425
Arlington, VA 22203

Standard reference number	Title	Referenced in code section number
210/240—94	Unitary Air-Conditioning and Air-Source Heat Pump Equipment	Table 503.2, Table 803.2.2(1), Table 803.2.2(2)
310/380—93	Packaged Terminal Air-Conditioners and Heat Pumps	202, Table 803.2.2(3)
320—98	Water-Source Heat Pumps	Table 803.2.2(2)
325—98	Ground Water-Source Heat Pumps	Table 803.2.2(2)
340/360—93	Commercial and Industrial Unitary Air-Conditioning and Heat Pump Equipment	Table 803.2.2(1), Table 803.2.2(2)
365—94	Commercial and Industrial Unitary Air-Conditioning Condensing Units	Table 803.3.2(1)
460—94	Remote Mechanical-Draft Air-Cooled Refrigerant Condensers	Table 803.2.2(6)
550/590—98	Water Chilling Packages Using the Vapor Compression Cycle	Table 803.3.2(2)

ASHRAE

American Society of Heating, Refrigerating and Air-Conditioning Engineers, Inc.
1791 Tullie Circle, NE
Atlanta, GA 30329-2305

Standard reference number	Title	Referenced in code section number
55—92	Thermal Environmental Conditions for Human Occupancy	202
62—99	Ventilation for Acceptable Indoor Air Quality	202
90.1—99	Energy Standard for Buildings Except Low-Rise Residential Buildings	701.1, 801.2, 802.1, 802.2
136—93	Method of Determining Air Change Rates in Detached Dwellings	402.1.3.10
ASHRAE—97	Handbook of Fundamentals	402.3.2, 502.2.1.1.2, 502.2.2, 502.2.3.1(1), 502.2.3.1(2), 503.3.1, 803.2.1
ASHRAE—99	HVAC Systems and Applications Handbook	504.2.2

ASME

American Society of Mechanical Engineers
Three Park Avenue
New York, NY 10016-5990

Standard reference number	Title	Referenced in code section number
A112.18.1M—96	Plumbing Fixture Fittings	504.6.1
ASME-PTC 4.1—1964	Steam Generating Units	Table 803.2.2(5)

ASTM

American Society for Testing and Materials
100 Barr Harbor Drive
West Conshohocken, PA 19428-2859

Standard reference number	Title	Referenced in code section number
C236—93^{E1}	Standard Test Method for Steady-State Thermal Performance of Building Assemblies by Means of a Guarded Hot Box	602.1.1.1
C 518—98	Standard Test Method for Steady-State Heat Flux Measurements and Thermal Transmission Properties by Means of the Heat Flow Meter Apparatus	Table 503.3.3.3
C976—96^{E1}	Standard Test Method for Thermal Performance of Building Assemblies by Means of a Calibrated Hot Box	602.1.1.1
D 4099—95	Standard Specification for Poly (Vinyl Chloride) PVC Prime Windows/Sliding Glass Doors	Table 502.1.4.1
E 96—95	Standard Test Methods for Water Vapor Transmission of Materials	502.1.1, 602.1.7, 802.1.2
E 283—91	Standard Test Method for Determining the Rate of Air Leakage Through Exterior Windows, Curtain Walls and Doors Under Specified Pressure Differences Across the Specimen	502.1.3, Table 502.1.4.1, 802.3.1
E 779—99	Standard Test Method for Determining Air Leakage Rate by Fan Pressurization	402.1.3.10

CTI

Cooling Tower Institute
530 Wells Fargo, Suite 218
Houston, TX 77090

Standard reference number	Title	Referenced in code section number
CTI ATC-105 (97)	Acceptance Test Code For Water Cooling Towers	Table 803.3.2(6)
CTI-201 (96)	Standard For Certification of Water Cooling Tower Thermal Performance	Table 803.3.2(6)

DOE

U.S. Department of Energy
c/o Superintendent of Documents
U.S. Government Printing Office
Washington, DC 20402-9325

Standard reference number	Title	Referenced in code section number
10 CFR; Part 430, Subpart B, Appendix E—98	Uniform Test Method for Measuring the Energy Consumption of Water Heaters	Table 504.2, Table 803.2.2(4)
10 CFR; Part 430, Subpart B, Appendix N—98	Uniform Test Method for Measuring the Energy Consumption of Furnaces	Table 503.2, Table 803.2.2(5)
10 CFR; Part 430, Subpart B, Test Procedures—98	Energy Conservation Program for Consumer Products	202
DOE—88	DOE Building Foundation Design Handbook	Table 502.2, 502.2.1.5, 502.2.3.5
DOE—Current Calendar Year	DOE State-Average Energy Prices	806.2.3

HI

Hydronics Institute
35 Russo Place
P.O. Box 218
Berkley Heights, NJ 07922

Standard reference number	Title	Referenced in code section number
HI HBS 86—89	Heating Boiler Standard 86 - Testing and Rating Standard for Heating Boilers, 6th Ed.	Table 803.2.2(5)

ICBO

International Conference of Building Officials
5360 Workman Mill Road
Whittier, CA 90601-2298

Standard reference number	Title	Referenced in code section number
BC—NYS—2002	Building Code of New York State	202
FC—NYS—2002	Fire Code of New York State	202
FGC—NYS—2002	Fuel Gas Code of New York State	202
MC—NYS—2002	Mechanical Code of New York State	202, 503.3.3.4, 803.2.5, 803.2.6, 803.3.4, 803.3.8.1
PC—NYS—2002	Plumbing Code of New York State	202

IESNA

Illuminating Engineering Society of North America
120 Wall Street, 17th Floor
New York, NY 10005-4001

Standard reference number	Title	Referenced in code section number
IESNA/ASHRAE 90.1—99	Energy Standard for Buildings Except Low-Rise Residential Buildings	701.1, 801.2, 802.1, 802.2

ISO

International Standards Organization
1, rue de Varembe,
Case postale 56,
CH - 1211 Geneve 20, Switzerland

Standard reference number	Title	Referenced in code section number
ISO 13256-1 (1998)	Water-Source Heat Pumps — Testing and Rating for Performance — Part 1: Water-to-Air and Brine-to-Air Heat Pumps	Table 803.2.2(2)

NFRC

National Fenestration Rating Council, Inc.
Suite 120
1300 Spring Street Park
Silver Spring, MD 20910

Standard reference number	Title	Referenced in code section number
100—97	Procedure for Determining Fenestration Product U-Factors	102.5.2, 601.3.2, 601.3.2.1
200—97	Procedure for Determining Fenestration Product Solar Heat Gain Coefficients at Normal Incidence	102.5.2, 601.3.2, 601.3.2.1

SMACNA

Sheet Metal and Air Conditioning Contractors National Association, Inc.
4021 Lafayette Center Drive
Chantilly, VA 20151-1209

Standard reference number	Title	Referenced in code section number
SMACNA—85	HVAC Air Duct Leakage Test Manual	402.1.3.9, 803.3.6

WDMA

Window and Door Manufacturers Association
1400 Touhy Avenue
Des Plaines, IL 60018

Standard reference number	Title	Referenced in code section number
101/I.S.2—97	Voluntary Specifications for Aluminum, Vinyl (PVC) and Wood Windows and Glass Doors	Table 502.1.4.1, 601.3.2.2, 802.3.1

UL

Underwriters Laboratories Inc.
333 Pfingsten Road
Northbrook, IL 60062-2096

Standard reference number	Title	Referenced in code section number
181A—94	Closure Systems for Use with Rigid Air Ducts and Air Connectors —with Revisions thru December 1998	503.3.3.4.3, 803.2.8
181B—95	Closure Systems for Use with Flexible Air Ducts and Air Connectors —with Revisions thru December 1998	503.3.3.4.3, 803.2.8
727—94	Oil-Fired Central Furnaces—with Revisions thru January 1999	Table 803.2.2(4)
731—95	Oil-Fired Unit Heaters—with Revisions thru January 1999	Table 803.2.2(4)

INDEX